The Standard & Poor's Guide
to Long-Term Investing

OTHER STANDARD & POOR'S BOOKS

*THE STANDARD & POOR'S GUIDE
FOR THE NEW INVESTOR*
by Nilus Mattive

*THE STANDARD & POOR'S GUIDE
TO SAVING AND INVESTING FOR COLLEGE*
by David J. Braverman

THE Standard & Poor's Guide to Long-Term Investing

JOSEPH R. TIGUE

McGRAW-HILL
New York | Chicago | San Francisco | Lisbon
London | Madrid | Mexico City | Milan | New Delhi
San Juan | Seoul | Singapore | Sydney | Toronto

The *McGraw·Hill* Companies

5 6 7 8 9 0   DOC/DOC   0 9 8 7 6 5

ISBN 0-07-141035-X

This book is printed on recycled, acid-free paper containing a minimum of 50% recycled de-inked paper.

Library of Congress Cataloging-in-Publication Data

Tigue, Joseph.
  The Standard & Poor's guide to long-term investing : 7 keys to
building wealth / by Joseph Tigue.
     p. cm.
  ISBN 0-07-141035-X (pbk. : alk. paper)
1. Investments—United States. 2. Portfolio management—United States. 3. Investment analysis. I. Title: Standard and Poor's guide to long-term investing. II. Title.
  HG4910.T54 2003
  332.6—dc21
                          2003012940

Contents

Preface

Throughout the 1990s investors were witness to the mother of all bull markets. The S&P 500 index, considered *the* market benchmark by professionals, soared 417 percent from October 12, 1990, to its peak on March 24, 2000 (from 1995 to 1999, the "500" was up at least 20% in each year). More spectacular was the performance of the Nasdaq, where many of the hot technology and Internet stocks are traded. That index rocketed upward more than 1400% from mid-October 1990 to mid-March 2000. Many stockholders became millionaires virtually overnight—though in many cases, only on paper. The subsequent market crash resulted in the greatest loss of wealth in investing history. About seven trillion dollars—more than five times the GDP of Russia—went down the drain, with euphoria turning to deep despair.

The bear market, which started in March 2000 and reached a low in early October 2002, took the S&P 500 down 49 percent. Nasdaq plunged 78 percent, the steepest decline for any major U.S. market index since the 1930s. The many revelations of corporate dishonesty—Enron, Arthur Andersen, Global Crossing, WorldCom, Xerox, and Tyco, to name the more infamous—also shook investor confidence. In 2002, the S&P 500 and Dow Jones Industrials fell for the third consecutive year, only the fourth time that has happened since 1900. Nevertheless, it's likely that stocks will continue to be the investment of choice over time. See Figure P-1.

The market's ups and downs notwithstanding, stocks should play a key role in helping you to reach your financial goals. Over the long term, stocks have outperformed other assets, including bonds, gold, and real estate by a wide margin. From 1928 to 2002, stocks, as measured by the S&P 500, delivered an average annual return of 11.9% (price changes plus dividends reinvested).

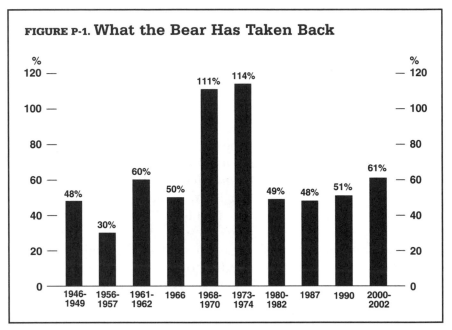

FIGURE P-1. What the Bear Has Taken Back

Every bear market of the last 56 years has taken back at least 30% of what the S&P 500 Index gained in the previous bull market.

The key term in any successful game plan is "stick-to-it-ness." No two ways about it, it's important that you continue to invest through thick and thin.

In the long run, bull markets have had more staying power than bear markets. Put more colorfully, the bulls always gore the bears. Bear markets, usually defined as at least a 20% decline in major stock indexes, such as the S&P 500 and Dow-Jones Industrials, are relatively few. Since the end of World War II, we've seen only ten of these down markets, with the average length a comparatively modest 16 months. Typically, stock market cycles are shorter and sharper in a bear phase than in an upswing, since selling tends to be concentrated and therefore relatively rapidly exhausted. The average loss in the last ten bear markets was 31%. On the other hand, the ten bull markets since World War II lasted an average of 56 months, with the gain averaging a hefty 155%.

Why do bull markets more than offset bear markets? Stocks reflect companies' underlying earning power, which tends to grow, on balance, over time. Corporate earnings increase because the economy expands for longer periods than it contracts. Since 1900, the economy was in a slump an average of 15 months, while the number of expansions averaged 43 months. Since 1945, recessions averaged 11 months and economic expansions averaged 59.

So don't be discouraged or be tempted to sell your stock positions when the market is in a downtrend. Keep buying the solid blue chips and mutual funds that are recommended in this book. The corny song from the musical *Annie* has a lot of truth to it: "Tomorrow, tomorrow, the sun will come out tomorrow."

Introduction

The plethora of investment information on the Internet, in books, newspapers, and magazines, as well as on TV and radio, often results in more confusion than clarification. The word *overload* comes immediately to mind.

The purpose of this book is to demystify and simplify the investing process. I believe that with a little study and due diligence, anyone can be their own investment advisor. You don't have to rely on stockbrokers or so-called financial planners. Many of these people are more interested in feathering their own nests than in giving you advice that is right for you in terms of your investment objectives, time horizon, and risk tolerance. A friend once told me he asked his father what investments he had purchased over the years. The father replied, "I never bought anything, but I was sold a lot!"

This book, in effect, sets forth an investment approach that has done well by me over the 40-odd years I've been in the stock market. Essentially, the program is a no-brainer, which some have said couldn't possibly work because it's too easy. The more complicated and arcane the investment process is made, it appears, the more successful many think it should be. My philosophy has always been: less is more. Why complicate things or gild the lily when simplicity usually is the best answer?

With the advent in 2000 of the worst bear market since the Great Depression, however, my "simplistic" approach seems to be slowly catching on. Investors have become painfully aware that following the crowd can have disastrous repercussions and that you have as much of a chance of getting rich quickly as the likelihood of a blizzard developing in the Sahara. As investors hopped onto the Internet/technology bandwagon, and as stock prices and valuations soared, the thinking was that this time it's different—trees indeed can grow to the sky. The subsequent loud bursting of the bubble that began in March 2000 proved that it's not different this time. It also showed that earnings do matter. Many of the Internet companies never earned a penny—the stocks were valued on revenues and pipe dreams. The bear market, moreover, should have reinforced this basic lesson: shares of companies that do have earnings but trade at 80, 90, or 100 times those profits should be sold, not bought or held.

You will see as you read this book that I advocate buying reasonably priced, dividend-paying stocks and solid mutual funds (preferably low-cost index funds) on a regular basis, which gives you the benefits of dollar cost averaging (see Chapter 6). Since most of us don't have the discipline to sit down and write a check each month to buy stocks and/or mutual funds, setting up an automatic investment plan, whereby money is taken out of your checking or banking account, is a must. Over the long term there is more risk in being out of the market than in it.

I sincerely believe that if you adopt these seven keys, you will reach your financial goals, and most important, you will do so worry-free:

Key 1—Pay Yourself First

Key 2—Hold Stocks for the Long Term

Key 3—Buy What You Know

Key 4—Dollar Cost Average

Key 5—Keep Your Costs Down

Key 6—Know When to Sell

Key 7—Start Now

There's nothing mysterious or complicated here. The same is true of the details on each of these seven keys, as well as on other important investment concepts and insights. The summary at the end of each chapter will help you to quickly review what you've learned. As you read this book, keep in mind that key number 7 is the master key—Start Now!

Acknowledgments

This book would not have been possible without the help and support of many of my former colleagues at Standard & Poor's. The ideas and critiques by Jim Dunn, a consultant for Standard & Poor's and former vice president and treasurer of GTE Corp., have been invaluable. The impressive graphics are the work of Chris Peng, who gathered the data, and LiWah Lai, Susanna Lee, Annabel Alafriz, and Debby Lee, whose talent and artistry can be seen in the charts and tables. Howard Silverblatt, Standard & Poor's datameister, is responsible for all the information on the S&P 500 index and the computer screens. His data massaging is without peer. Mark Arbter, S&P's chief market technician, supplied the charts illustrating technical analysis.

McGraw-Hill Professional Book Group editor Kelli Christiansen kept me on course and came up with on-target suggestions. Thanks also goes to Jeffrey Krames, vice president, McGraw-Hill Professional Book Group and bestselling author, who got the ball rolling, and to the members of the Standard & Poor's Press Committee: George Gulla, James Branscome, and Shari Stein.

My wife, Barbara, and three daughters, Melissa, Elizabeth, and Barbara Susan, encouraged and supported me in this endeavor. And to use a well-worn expression, "last but not least," special thanks to Arnold Kaufman, former long-time editor of Standard & Poor's weekly investment advisory flagship newsletter *The Outlook*, for his market insights and to Joe Lisanti, current editor-in-chief of *The Outlook* and co-author with me of *The Dividend Rich Investor*, for his encouragement. Thanks again to S&P vice president George Gulla, whose enthusiasm for the project rubbed off on all of us.

CHAPTER 1

The First Key: Pay Yourself First

We all have to sit down each and every month and pay our bills: mortgage or rent, gas, electric, telephone, car payment, credit cards, and so on. It's not exactly a picnic in the park. But how many of us ever consider *paying ourselves* before we write checks to First Homestead Bank or Allpower Energy?

Paying yourself first simply means saving or investing on a *regular* basis. It's certainly not a new concept, but if you follow it faithfully, you'll wind up financially successful. The number one rule for meeting your long-term investment goals—and its importance can't be emphasized enough—is to set up a plan whereby money periodically goes into some kind of a savings account.

If you or your spouse have a 401(k) or similar plan at work, this should be funded first, especially if your company matches your contributions. But even if there is no match, putting money into a 401(k) each payday makes sense from three standpoints: (1) You reduce your taxes, since contributions are pretax, (2) you enjoy the benefits of tax deferral, and your money goes in on a dollar cost averaging basis (which we'll discuss in Chapter 6), and (3) your money grows tax free, which boosts the power of compounding.

Compounding, which will be emphasized throughout the book, is often preceded by the words "magic of." It's the way your investment increases as it earns a return on the initial money you invested and on the interest or dividends earned. When Albert Einstein was asked what the most important thing he learned from mathematics was, he

FIGURE 1-1. **The Power of Compounding***

Year	Early Funding Contribution	Year-end Value	Late Funding Contribution	Year-end Value
1	$2,000	$2,200	$0	$0
2	2,000	4,620	0	0
3	2,000	7,282	0	0
4	2,000	10,210	0	0
5	2,000	13,431	0	0
6	2,000	16,974	0	0
7	2,000	20,871	0	0
8	2,000	25,158	0	0
9	0	27,674	2,000	2,200
10	0	30,441	2,000	4,620
11	0	33,485	2,000	7,282
12	0	36,834	2,000	10,210
13	0	40,517	2,000	13,431
14	0	44,569	2,000	16,974
15	0	49,026	2,000	20,871
16	0	53,929	2,000	25,158
17	0	59,322	2,000	29,874
18	0	65,254	2,000	35,061
19	0	71,779	2,000	40,767
20	0	78,957	2,000	47,044
21	0	86,853	2,000	53,948
22	0	95,583	2,000	61,643
23	0	105,092	2,000	69,897
24	0	115,601	2,000	79,087
25	0	127,161	2,000	89,196
26	0	139,877	2,000	100,316
27	0	153,865	2,000	112,548
28	0	169,252	2,000	126,003
29	0	186,177	2,000	140,803
30	0	204,795	2,000	157,083
31	0	225,275	2,000	174,991
32	0	247,803	2,000	194,690
33	0	272,583	2,000	216,359
34	0	299,841	2,000	240,195
35	0	329,825	2,000	266,415
36	0	362,808	2,000	295,257
37	0	399,089	2,000	326,983
38	0	438,998	2,000	361,881
39	0	482,898	2,000	400,269
40	0	531,188	2,000	442,496

*If you invest $2,000 a year for only the first 10 years of a 40-year period with annual compounding at 8%, you will earn more than someone who invests $2,000 a year from years 10 through 40. The latter's total contribution would be 3 times greater, yet would earn 31% less.

replied, "Compound interest; it's the most powerful force on earth." The power of compounding is illustrated in Figure 1-1.

If you put $500 into an account that pays 8 percent a year, compounded annually, and you don't make any further contributions, you would have $2300 at the end of 20 years. Or, consider this example of saving regularly: An investment of $500 a year earning 8 percent will grow to $22,881 in 20 years, compounded annually. You will have invested only $10,000 in that time, but your investment will grow an additional $12,881.

Here's an even more dramatic example: A 21-year-old with a 401(k) who puts in only $800 each year and earns 8 percent annually will contribute a total of $34,400 at the retirement age of 67. The whole investment, however, will have grown to $284,760. If the employer matched contributions, the worker will have $569,520 by the time he or she retires.

Rule of 72

To find out how long it would take to double your money at different rates, divide 72 by the yield. If you earn 6 percent, for example, it will take 12 years to double your money (72/6 = 12); at 7 percent it will take 10 years; at 8 percent, nine years; and so on. Or, say you borrowed $1000 from a friend who is charging 6 percent interest.

FIGURE 1-2. Compounding: The Rule of 72

Year	Starting $ Amount	Earnings	Ending $ Amount
1	1,000	80	1,080
2	1,080	86	1,166
3	1,166	93	1,259
4	1,259	101	1,360
5	1,360	109	1,469
6	1,469	117	1,586
7	1,586	127	1,713
8	1,713	137	1,850
9	1,850	148	1,998

Divide 72 by 6; you get 12, which is the number of years it would take for your debt to double to $2000 if you didn't make any payments. See Figure 1-2 on page 3, for the way the Rule of 72 works using a $1000 investment returning 8 percent annually.

Let's get greedy. To find out how long it takes to triple your money, use the Rule of 115. Divide the rate of return into 115. For example, an investment earning an 8 percent return will triple in 14 years.

The point is, compounding plays a pivotal role in building wealth.

Save, Save, Save

Even if you're contributing the maximum to a 401(k)—which the IRS calls a defined *contribution* plan—it doesn't mean you're home free. Most companies these days don't have pensions—or defined *benefit* plans—so when you retire, the chances are that you won't be able to rely on a steady stream of income each month, as your parents and grandparents did. Given longer life expectancies, you have no choice but to supplement your Social Security (which one hopes will still be around) and 401(k) with a regular savings plan. And "regular" doesn't mean every quarter or twice a year.

Individual Retirement Accounts

In fact, we believe that you should set up a weekly or monthly investment plan. To start, open a tax-deferred plan such as a traditional Individual Retirement Account (IRA). If both you and your spouse work and have taxable compensation, each of you can contribute up to $3000 to a separate traditional IRA. Even if one spouse has little or no compensation, up to $3000 can be contributed to each IRA if combined compensation is at least equal to the amount contributed to both IRAs and you file a joint return. If you file a joint return, you can contribute $3000 to a separate IRA for your nonworking spouse.

The maximum traditional IRA contribution in the years 2005-2007 will rise to $4000, and for 2008 and thereafter, it will climb to $5000. For those who have reached the age of 50, the maximum contribution is $3500 annually for the tax years 2002 through 2004; $4500 for 2005; $5000 for 2006 and 2007; and $6000 for 2008 and thereafter.

Under certain circumstances, moreover, your contributions to a traditional IRA may be tax deductible. If you have earned income and are not in an employer-sponsored retirement plan, you can deduct your contributions; or even if you're in an employer-sponsored pension plan, you can take a full deduction if you and your spouse file jointly and your adjusted gross income (AGI) is under $60,000 (for 2003; the amount increases each year, reaching $80,000 in 2005). Single filers may deduct their contributions if their AGI is under $40,000 (for 2003; the amount increases each year, reaching $50,000 in 2005).

Roth IRAs

For those who qualify, a Roth IRA is a better deal. While contributions are not tax deductible with the Roth, if you're over age 59$^{1/2}$ and have been in the Roth for at least five years you don't pay taxes when you withdraw the money.

As with a traditional IRA, you're eligible to make a regular contribution to a Roth IRA even if you participate in an employer retirement plan. These contributions can be as much as $3000 ($3500 if you're 50 or older), which will increase each year, reaching $5000 in 2008 (or $6000 if you are 50 or older). There are just two requirements: You or your spouse must have compensation or alimony income equal to the amount contributed, and your modified adjusted gross income can't exceed certain limits. For the maximum contribution, the limits are $95,000 for single individuals and $150,000 for married individuals filing joint returns. The amount you can contribute is reduced gradually and then completely eliminated when your modified adjusted gross income exceeds $110,000 (single) or $160,000 (married filing jointly).

Many have recognized the value of and the need for IRA accounts. From 1999 to 2002, the number of households with an IRA jumped from 30 to 40 percent. Since 1990, the total assets in IRAs have surged 278 percent, to $2.4 trillion, despite the poor 2000–2002 stock market. These numbers are encouraging, but it's still a fact that only about half of all Americans save.

With traditional pension plans going the way of the dodo, retiree health-care benefits as scarce as a successful hot stock tip, and Social Security on less than firm ground, it's imperative that you set up an IRA account as early as possible, as part of your plan to pay yourself first.

A tax-deferred IRA account lets your money increase faster by delaying the payment of taxes. If you invest $1000 a year in an IRA or a 401(k) that returns 8 percent annually, in 30 years your money will grow to $122,346 before taxes, compared with only $74,485 in a taxable account.

New Savings Proposals

In early 2003, President Bush proposed two new consolidated savings accounts—Lifetime Savings Accounts (LSAs) and Retirement Savings Accounts (RSAs)—that would allow everyone to contribute, with no limitations based on age or income status. Individuals could convert existing accounts into the new accounts. The savings plans are an attempt to simplify the maze of deferred-tax plans—from 401(k)s to 529s for college—converting them to a Roth-style structure where contributions are not deductible but withdrawals are not taxed.

The LSAs, which could be accessed at any time without penalty, would replace college savings and other plans. Contributions would not need to be from earned income. The RSAs would replace IRAs and other personal retirement plans. The Employee Retirement Savings Plan (ERSA) would replace the 401(k), 403(b), and other employer-sponsored plans. The limits are raised very sharply—to $7500 per person for the LSAs and RSAs, and $15,000 for ERSAs. A working couple could sock away as much as $60,000 per year in a combination of all three plans, and more if they have children.

At this writing, chances are not good for passage of these proposals, though some form of the plan may be adopted eventually. If only half of the $2.4 trillion in IRAs is converted into RSAs—on which taxes would have to be paid—the Treasury would collect $250 billion.

A No-Brainer: Invest Automatically

Over the years, I've found the best way to set up a regular investment plan—be it tax deferred or not—is to have money automatically taken out of my checking or savings account. As they say, what you don't see, you don't miss. This no-brainer method prevents you from blowing money on stuff you really don't need. The money each month should go into no-load (no sales charge) mutual funds and stocks that can be purchased directly from the companies (we'll discuss this in Chapter 7). At the very least, your money each month should be put into a certificate of deposit (CD) or a money market account as a way to save for your first mutual fund or stock investment.

The natural response to setting up an automatic investment plan is, "I can't afford it." The truth is you can't afford *not* to do it.

Ways to Save

The key to investing on a regular basis—and to your financial health—is to live beneath (not beyond) your means. Here are a few helpful hints. You've probably heard most of them before, but this time put them to work!

LOTTERY TICKETS ARE NOT A WAY TO TAKE CARE OF YOURSELF IN THE GOLDEN YEARS. Despite the commercials (you've got to be in it to win it) and the stories of winners who didn't have a pot to put flowers in, you have a better chance of being struck by lightning than taking home the big jackpot. Even though you may spend only a couple of dollars on the lottery each week, that money adds up and is diverting funds from your investment portfolio, which lengthens your time horizon for your financial freedom.

Warren Buffett, legendary investor and the second richest man in the United States after Microsoft's Bill Gates, has this to say about gambling: "The propensity to gamble is always increased by a large prize versus a small entry fee, no matter how poor the true odds may be. That's why Las Vegas casinos advertise big jackpots and why state lotteries headline big prizes." Further, he says: "People would rather be promised a (presumably) winning lottery ticket next week than an opportunity to get rich slowly."

Your motto should be: I'd rather be tortoise rich than a hare wannabe millionaire.

KEEP TRACK OF YOUR SPENDING. By writing down where the money goes, you'll discover where you're spending foolishly. You should also do some research and find out what percentage of your income you're spending on each item. If, for example, you take home $3000 each month and you pay $1000 on your mortgage, divide $1000 by $3000, which amounts to 33 percent. In this way, you can see where you're spending too much and, where practical, you can reduce the percentage gradually.

DON'T SPEND YOUR CHANGE. Every night, empty out your pants pockets or pocketbooks and put the loose change into a jar or piggy bank. I do this, and you'd be surprised how quickly the pennies, nickels, dimes, and quarters add up. In a couple of months you may have enough to buy a share of a stock or of a mutual fund.

IT'S FUN TO EAT OUT—BUT EXPENSIVE. If you want to treat yourself and your spouse or friend, why not order take-out? You'll save on the tip and a substantial amount of money on drinks, which are inevitably overpriced at restaurants. According to the U.S. Bureau of Labor Statistics, the average household (with income of $45,000) spends over $2000 eating out each year. By ordering in—and also by cutting back on the number of times you eat take-out food—you could save at least half of that amount.

IF YOU'RE NOT ENTERTAINING CLIENTS, BRING YOUR LUNCH TO WORK. Even though you may only spend six dollars a day on lunch, that adds up to $120 a month.

DON'T TRY TO IMPRESS YOUR FRIENDS WITH PRICEY VACA-TIONS. You can have just as good a time—or better—at a spot close to home. There are bound to be some interesting areas nearby. If not, what's wrong with going to a fancy hotel with all the amenities and just hanging out? If you can go off-season, that's even better. It's outrageous what hotels and resorts charge in season. Visiting a nearby National Park also is an enjoyable, inexpensive way to vacation (see the website www.nps.gov).

SAVE MONEY ON AUTO AND HOME INSURANCE: UP YOUR DEDUCTIBLES. Put a few dollars away in a savings account to cover the deductibles rather than paying onerous rates for smaller deductibles. Also, compare auto insurance rates every year and stop collision and comprehensive coverage on cars that are five years or older. Take a defensive driving course, which will cut rates by at least 5 percent.

NEVER BUY WHOLE LIFE INSURANCE. A 40-year-old woman, for example, who buys a $250,000 whole life policy pays about $3275 annually. The insurance agent gets a commission of around $2290 the first year and more than $300 each year the policy is in force. So, unless you want to line the pockets of an insurance agent, term life insurance is your best bet. You can get a lot of coverage for a very reasonable price.

NEVER BUY A VARIABLE ANNUITY. Essentially a contract between the buyer and an insurance company under which the insurer agrees to make periodic payments, variable annuities typically are invested in mutual funds. The fees can amount to as much as 2 percent of your holdings each year; that is, on a $40,000 account you would pay $800 annually. Also, it often takes at least 15 years before the performance of the annuity matches the after-tax returns of investments in a taxable account, so the money is tied up for a long time. Moreover, the "death benefit," which will pay your beneficiaries at least as much as you put into the annuity, can cost more than it's worth. You'll also have to pay a "surrender charge" if you withdraw money within a certain period after purchase, typically within six to eight years, but sometimes as long as 10 years. And if you don't withdraw the money before you die, your beneficiaries will be taxed on it. A pretty lousy deal all around.

BEFORE MAKING MAJOR PURCHASES, DO RESEARCH. Get the best buys from *Consumer Reports* magazine, which can be found in your local library. Don't be shy about negotiating prices. Another good source is the website www.pricegrabber.com, on which you can comparison shop.

When you buy a new car, you pay the retail price. As soon as you drive it off the lot, it depreciates; that is, it's worth its wholesale price. And then a typical car loses 15 to 20 percent of its value each year. A car that's two years old will be worth 80 percent to 85 percent of its one-year value. A three-year-old car will be about 80 percent to 85 percent of its two-year value. A used car, therefore, is a better bet, especially with so many of them coming off leases each year, and with most still on warranty.

You can get all kinds of information on a car you're interested in buying via websites www.carfaxreport.com and www.auto.consumerguide.com. Just type in the vehicle identification number (VIN) to find out if the car has been in a major accident or if the odometer was turned back. Also check out www.bluebook.com, www.carprice.com, and www.nadaguides.com for pricing information and shopping and negotiating tips.

IF POSSIBLE, FILL YOUR GAS TANK WITH REGULAR GAS. Studies show that less than 10 percent of cars on the road require premium gas, but 20 percent of all gas consumed is premium. The more expensive gas does not give you better mileage, and only such high-performance cars as Mercedes or BMWs—which you shouldn't buy anyway, unless you have money to burn—need premium gas.

ALWAYS PAY CREDIT CARD BILLS AS THEY COME DUE. At the end of 2002, the average credit card debt for households with at least one credit card was $8367, and the average interest rate for a standard card was 17 percent. Typically, people try to pay off that debt by making the minimum monthly payment. The problem is, interest is paid on both the amounts charged and on the unpaid interest owed. If you make only the minimum monthly payments on $8367, it would take more than 22 years to pay it off and would cost you $10,284 in interest. If you pay the minimum amounts due plus an additional $100 each month, you could erase the debt in less than five years, at a cost of $3193.

More states should follow California's lead and pass a law requiring credit card bills to carry this warning: "Making only the minimum payment will increase the interest you pay and the time it takes to repay your balance." The law also requires card issuers to spell out how much interest and time would be required to pay off typical balances at 17 percent, making only minimum payments of 2 percent. A balance of $1000, for example, would cost $2590 over 17 years and three months. To pay off $2500 would cost $7773 and take 30 years and three months.

Your house is probably the only asset that should be bought on time. For one thing, the mortgage interest is deductible on your taxes, and for another, your investment becomes more valuable over the years via equity build-up. Be aware that when interest rates are falling, as was the case in 2000–2003, it's time to reassess your mortgage. As a rule of thumb, if your mortgage rate is at least 2 percentage points higher than the prevailing rate, you may want to refinance. You could save hundreds of dollar a month with a lower rate.

NEVER BUY ANYTHING JUST BECAUSE IT'S ON SALE. And never consider shopping a recreational activity. Avoid impulse buying. Paying yourself first doesn't mean spending for yourself first.

MAKE THE MOST OF YOUR LOCAL LIBRARY. Why spend money on books (except the one you're reading now), CDs, and videotapes when you can take them out of your library for free? Once you've purchased these costly items, how often do you revisit them?

WHEN IT'S TIME FOR COLLEGE, CONSIDER STATE SCHOOLS. Most of them are just as good—or better—than private schools. What counts in getting a good job, when you're considering your children or grandchildren, are the grades.

The cost differential between state and private schools is considerable. According to the College Board, for the school year 2002–2003 average tuition for a four-year private college was $18,273 (books, fees, and living expenses not included) versus $4081 for a four-year public college. The average surcharge for out-of-state or out-of-district students at public institutions is $6347 at four-year colleges. Of course, you should also check out what's available in the way of student aid or student loans. Often, you can negotiate a college's "sticker price."

It's also a good idea to look into community colleges. It's much cheaper to attend a two-year college and then transfer to a four-year college to earn a B.A. or a B.S.

SAVE YOUR RAISE. When you get a salary increase (most people get one every year), up the money you save each month by at least half the amount of the raise. Guaranteed, you'll hardly miss it, and it will make a big difference in your financial well-being.

These are just a few suggestions on saving money. I'm sure you can come up with more if you put on your thinking cap. So no excuses. You *can* and *must* pay yourself first. Set up those automatic investment plans now.

You'll discover that being financially disciplined gives you a euphoric sense of freedom and sets you on the right path for successful, long-term investing.

Points to Remember

- ➤ Each and every month, pay yourself first. Either have an automatic savings plan set up or write a check for investments.

- ➤ Don't say you can't afford a regular savings program. You can't afford *not* to have one.

- ➤ Keep track of your spending.

- ➤ Follow the various suggestions on spending less, such as not buying lottery tickets, eating out less often, curbing your shopping, not spending your change, and boosting your insurance deductibles. Live below rather than above your means.

- ➤ Pay credit card bills fully and promptly.

- ➤ When thinking college, think state or community.

- ➤ When you get a salary increase, boost the amount of your savings by at least half that amount.

CHAPTER 2

Fear, Loathing, and Diversification on Wall Street

Investors, one hopes, have learned at least one important lesson from the so-called tech wreck of 2000, when stocks of those technology companies that were part of the "new economy" melted down. Cases in point: Cisco Systems, the leading supplier of networking equipment and network managing for the Internet, plummeted from a high of $82 in 2000 to a measly $1.00. The shares of the quintessential new economy company, CMGI, which operates a network of Internet companies and manages venture capital funds that invest in Internet and tech companies, skidded to less than 30 cents in 2002 from a high of $163 in 2000. *Ouch!*

Tech investors finally realized that they had ignored one of the most basic tenets of investing: diversification. Putting all your eggs in one basket can lead to a scrambled mess of an investment portfolio and jeopardize your financial future.

Nowhere was this point driven home more forcefully than at that notorious place of business where few understood what kind of business it was in—Enron. The Houston-based company, formed in 1985, quickly mushroomed into the nation's seventh-largest corporation in terms of revenues by buying electricity from generators and selling it to consumers. Enron was considered an innovative company, though most of its innovation, it turned out, was in its accounting.

[13]

The company used complex partnerships to keep $500 million in debt off the books and mask its financial problems so it could continue to get cash and credit to run its trading business. Company officials admitted that Enron overstated its profits by more than $580 million from 1997 to 2001. After heavy losses, the company filed for protection from creditors in late 2001. It was the biggest corporate bankruptcy in U.S. history. The mere mention of Enron still brings chills to many, especially its employees. They lost millions of dollars in their 401(k) plans, as the stock plunged from $90 to pennies a share. Top Enron executives, meanwhile, cashed out more than $1 billion in the stock when it was near its peak.

The Benefits of Diversification

Sticking with a diversified investment program over many years can overcome short-term market declines and also reduce risk and/or volatility. According to a study by Jeremy Siegel, professor of finance at the University of Pennsylvania's Wharton School and author of *Stocks for the Long Run*, stocks held over the long term on an inflation-adjusted basis are less risky than bonds and Treasury bills, which are considered safe investments (see Chapter 10 for our take on bonds). Over the 20- and 30-year periods cited in his study, which went back to 1802, stocks were no more volatile than bonds or T-bills, and, unlike those so-called fixed-income assets, they never lost ground to inflation.

Specifically, diversification means to spread investments among different types of securities and various companies in different industries and sectors. Asset allocation, which we'll go into more in the next chapter, is diversifying a portfolio among different asset classes, which include stocks, bonds, cash (a money market fund is considered cash, as well as short-term certificates of deposit), and real estate and gold. Each asset class generally has a different level of return and risk, and each behaves differently. One asset may be rising in value, while another may be declining or not going up as much.

Diversification can be tricky for investors. You can own many stocks and mutual funds and still not be diversified if all of the securities are in similar asset classes, since the classes tend to move in the same direction. Thus, you should own at least two different classes—stocks and bonds—since they don't always rise and fall in value at the same time.

You should also diversify within the asset classes. For example, with stocks, make sure you have some in large-capitalization issues (capitalization is simply the number of shares outstanding times the price of the stock), mid-caps, and small-caps, as well as foreign issues.

Large- and Small-Cap Defined

Large-cap stocks are those with market capitalizations of more than $5 billion. Small-caps are less than $1 billion. And medium-caps are everything in between.

Large-caps, which include such giants as IBM, Microsoft, General Electric, ExxonMobil, Wal-Mart, and Pfizer, are generally more stable because bigger companies tend to have a stronger competitive position in their particular field of operation and a longer earnings and dividend history. At the same time, large-cap stocks are easy to trade—they're "liquid," in Wall Street parlance—since a large number of shares are bought and sold every day, and prices don't fluctuate as widely as those of smaller companies.

Smaller companies, in comparison, tend to increase earnings at a faster pace than large-cap companies. Generally, they're nimbler and can usually adjust to changing market conditions better than their larger brethren. But since there often is less demand for the shares of smaller companies, the group experiences more volatile price swings. Some examples of small-cap companies include Commerce Bancorp, a New Jersey regional bank; Scholastic Corp., a leading publisher and distributor of children's books and classroom and professional magazines; and Constellation Brands, a major U.S. producer of alcoholic beverages.

Here's a good instance of how diversification among different capitalization sizes is beneficial: In 2000 and 2001, the large-cap S&P 500 index fell 10 and 13 percent respectively (after racking up high-double-digit returns in the late 1990s), while the S&P SmallCap 600 index rose 11 and 5.7 percent respectively. In 2002, the large-cap 500 lost 23 percent, while the SmallCap index dropped only 15 percent. The S&P MidCap 400 index climbed 16.2 percent in 2000, dipped less than 2 percent in 2001, and fell 15 percent in 2002 (see Figures 2-1 and 2-2). So if your portfolio contained small- and mid-cap stocks in the market's 2000–2002 dive, your returns would have been far better than those of the large-cap S&P 500 index.

If mutual funds are more to your liking than individual stocks, then diversify with large-cap growth funds, small- and medium-cap funds, so-called value and growth funds, and foreign funds. Actually, to be truly diversified, you should have a mix of both stocks and mutual funds in your portfolio, as well as fixed-income securities. We'll have more to say about these different investments later on.

FIGURE 2-1. Larger Capitalization Companies vs. Smaller Capitalization Companies

Large Cap (at Least $5 Billion)	Mid Cap/Small Cap
Economies of scale	Greater earnings growth potential
Greater market liquidity	
Brand recognition	Do better coming out of recession
Market dominance	
More diversified	Less efficiently priced
Less dependent on one product	May be acquired at premium price
Greater management depth	Less subject to government and/or other growth impediments
More analytical coverage	
Stronger financials	More innovative

The bottom line: A blend of these stocks is best.

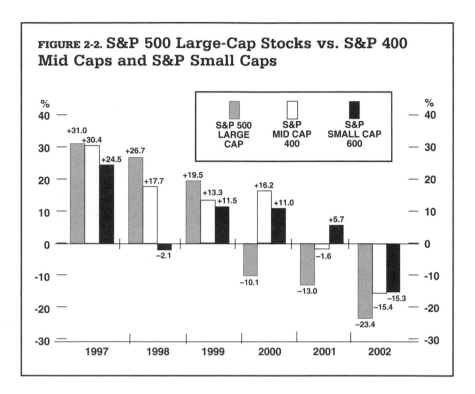

FIGURE 2-2. **S&P 500 Large-Cap Stocks vs. S&P 400 Mid Caps and S&P Small Caps**

Past Abuses ...

As mentioned earlier, the market's steep downturn in 2000–2002 was exacerbated by various accounting and insider trading scandals. Deceptive accounting practices at Enron and telecom companies Global Crossing and WorldCom resulted in their downfall. All three had the backing of their auditor, Arthur Andersen.

Lucent Technologies, spun off from AT&T and one of the most widely held stocks, booked more than $600 million in revenues from sales to its distributors before the distributors actually sold the products. Xerox was accused of inflating revenues by $3 billion from 1997 to 2000 and agreed to restate earnings for those years. WorldCom hid more than $7 million in expenses. Waste Management, the largest waste hauling firm in the United States, allegedly used fraudulent accounting to puff up earnings by more than $1.5 billion between 1992 and 1997. Guess who the auditor was?

The skulduggery wasn't limited to U.S. corporations. In early 2003, Dutch food retailer Royal Ahold NV, owner of Stop & Shop, Giant, and other supermarket chains, admitted that it had overstated earnings by at least $500 million. The resultant plunge in the company's stock of more than 70 percent, and the devaluation of its bonds to junk status, placed a pall over Ahold.

One of the deadliest of the seven deadly sins—greed—was the primary motivation behind the corporate chicanery. Nothing new, but as Federal Reserve Chairman Alan Greenspan said, "It is not that humans have become any more greedy than in generations past. It is that the avenues to express greed had grown so enormously."

... Hopefully Will Be Held in Check

These avenues to express greed, fortunately, were cut short by passage of the Sarbanes-Oxley Act of 2002. The important new bill created a regulatory board to oversee the accounting industry and discipline corrupt auditors.

The Securities & Exchange Commission, which has increased its budget and sharpened its watchdog skills, oversees the Public Company Accounting Oversight Board, as it's called. The board consists of five financially literate members appointed for five-year terms. Two of the members must be certified public accountants (CPAs) and the remaining three must not be and can not have been CPAs. No member may share in any of the profits of, or receive payments from, a public accounting firm, other than fixed continuing payments, such as those for retirement. Also, accountants are prohibited from offering a broad range of consulting services to publicly traded companies they audit. At the same time, accounting firms are required to change the lead on coordinating partners for a company every five years.

The board's duties:

1. Register public accounting firms.

2. Establish, or adopt, by rule, auditing, quality control, ethics, independence and other standards relating to the preparation of audit reports for issuers.

3. Conduct inspections of accounting firms.

4. Conduct investigations and disciplinary proceedings, and impose appropriate sanction.

5. Perform such other duties or functions as necessary or appropriate.

6. Enforce compliance with the act, the rules of the board, professional standards and the securities laws relating to the preparation and issuance of audit reports and the obligation and liabilities of accountants.

7. Set the budget and manage the operations of the board and the board's staff.

The legislation also toughened up corporate governance. Chief executives and chief financial officers of publicly traded companies must certify their financial statements each quarter. If they allow materially misleading information into the reports, they will face up to 20 years in jail. In addition, the bill prevents company executives from obtaining loans that are not available to outsiders. A number of executives had borrowed money from their companies and never paid them back.

Stock options played a large part in the accounting scandals, since the executives involved were mainly interested in boosting earnings so they could exercise their options and reap quick gains. Options are not considered an expense by most companies, which is absurd, since they are a form of compensation. Fortunately, many large corporations have capitulated and have begun expensing them, thanks, in part, to pressure by Standard & Poor's and by investor guru Warren Buffett. In early 2003, more than 100 companies were treating options as an expense of doing business, up from a handful in 2002 and from virtually none prior to that.

Standard & Poor's Core Earnings

Spurred by the many questionable practices, Standard & Poor's, in 2002, developed an approach for companies to report the earnings of their principal, or core, businesses. S&P's objectives were to provide consistency and transparency to earnings analyses and make it easier for investors to form comparisons between companies and over different time periods.

A growing number of companies prior to 2002 were using "pro forma" or "operating" earnings when they felt that net income as defined by generally accepted accounting principles (GAAP) did not give an accurate picture of their profits. Both pro forma and operating earnings are commonly profits that exclude special charges, such as asset write-downs and goodwill, which is the difference between the purchase price of an acquired company and its book value. However, these alternative earnings measures were rarely defined. Moreover, even when they were defined, the alternative profit measures varied from company to company, and often from one time period to another for the same company.

Figure 2-3, below, shows the differences between operating earnings (profits from operations, excluding special charges), as-reported earnings (what the company reports), and S&P's core earnings. The core earnings include stock option expenses, restructuring charges and write-offs, as well as purchased research and development.

FIGURE 2-3. Core Earnings Differences

	Operating Earnings	As-Reported Earnings	S&P Core Earnings
Stock Option Expense	Excluded	Excluded	Included
Pension Expense	Included	Included	Excludes pension fund gains & includes cost of service and interest
Goodwill	Excluded	Excluded unless impaired	Excluded
Restructuring Charges and writeoffs	Excluded	Included	Included
Purchased R&D	Excluded	Included	Included

Pension expense is also included in S&P's core earnings, as it is in operating earnings and as-reported earnings. But S&P's core earnings excludes pension fund gains and includes service and interest cost.

When an employee is covered by a pension plan, the annual service cost is the increase in the present value of the future pension obligations due to an added year of service and salary. That is, as each year passes and the time when future benefit obligations must be paid approaches, the present value of those obligations increases due to the interest cost. If the pension fund is properly managed and the stock market is doing reasonably well, the fund should earn enough each year to cover the annual interest costs. However, if the fund consistently fails to cover the interest cost, it will become more underfunded over time. In most years, it's likely that the majority of companies will cover their interest costs with the actual returns on the plan. But in some periods, as in down stock markets, the comparison of interest costs and actual returns results in added charges against S&P's core earnings.

One result of this treatment of interest costs and actual plan returns is to increase the apparent volatility of a company's earnings by incorporating market-generated results in the calculation. In theory, this would be avoided by replacing the actual return with an expected return or a moving average extending over several years. But as the stock market's performance in the last decade or so has demonstrated, this could easily leave analysts with earnings that concealed significant pension funding questions.

To avoid the apparent volatility that this treatment of pension interest costs may introduce, Standard & Poor's core earnings calculations excludes interest costs and shows them instead as a separate item, so analysts can exclude them if they wish. In effect, this is the same as assuming the pension plan can cover the interest costs. S&P's core earnings. Of course, in most years with modest gains in the stock market, this is not expected to be an issue.

Because of passage of the Sarbanes-Oxley Act and Standard & Poor's core earnings, which have led the way to sensible financial reporting, long-term investors should now gain more confidence in the companies in which they put their money, and have more faith in the market as a whole. Despite the bear market, corporate scandals, and a troubling global picture that launched this decade, new procedures and tools abound to help investors protect their wealth for the long term.

In the next chapter, we'll talk about the second key to financial success—holding stocks for the long term.

Points to Remember

➤ In real estate, the byword is location. In investing, it's diversification. You should own a mix of large-, small-, and medium-cap stocks and mutual funds, as well as some fixed-income securities (bonds). At the same time, you should not be too diversified, since you likely wouldn't have the money or time to buy and follow more than 15 stocks and funds.

➤ Have confidence in the stock market. The abuses and accounting chicanery witnessed in the roaring bull market of the late 1990s are being addressed, and it's likely we won't see a repeat—at least to that extent.

CHAPTER 3

The Second Key: Hold Stocks for the Long Term

The merits of long-term investing were forcibly brought home during the technology/dot-com bubble of the late 1990s. Making money in the market was as easy as shooting fish in a barrel (to use a phrase that's fresh as a daisy), which attracted hordes of people who left their steady, safe jobs to become day traders. Few of these in-and-out investors (sorry, make that "speculators") did well. In fact, more than 75 percent lost money, according to a study by the General Accounting Office and the Senate Permanent Subcommittee on Investigations, learning the hard way that short-term trading rarely leads to long-term success.

Even some of the brokerage houses that profited from day traders called it quits. In 2002, Merrill Lynch pulled the plug on its two-year-old $1 billion online bank and brokerage joint venture with global banking giant HSBC Holdings. In the same year, Morgan Stanley sold its online trading accounts to Bank of Montreal and Credit Suisse First Boston shed its online brokerage unit. Stock trades via the Internet fell to less than 15 percent of overall volume in U.S. equity markets in 2002, down from 30 percent in 2000.

Some traders, of course, can and do profit. But in order to make a decent return, they need to spend a great deal of time buying and selling stocks under tremendous pressure. Many buy on margin—purchasing stock with money borrowed from your broker—which can be a high-risk proposition. The monetary cost of short-term trading is not cheap either, since commissions and taxes can take a big slice of any gains.

A study by the University of California compared long-term investors and active traders. Some 20 percent of the investors in the study were traders. The buy-and-hold investors made few or no changes to their portfolios between 1991 and 1997, while the active traders changed their entire portfolio every year. The traders' annual returns in the period averaged only 11.4 percent, compared with the 18.5 percent enjoyed by the patient buy-and-hold crowd.

Charles Ellis, president of Greenwich Research and author of *Winning the Loser's Game*, puts it succinctly when he says that "investors must understand the turbulent nature of markets in the short term and the basic consistency of markets in the long term." And Peter Lynch, former manager of Fidelity's highly successful Magellan mutual fund, has said, "I have no feeling for the direction of the market over the near term or over the next three to 12 months—and that has always been my position."

A pivotal benefit of long-term investing is cost savings. When you're in the market for the long haul, you save on commissions and on taxes. Don't let anyone try to tell you that investment costs aren't that meaningful in the scheme of things. It's true that stock commissions have come way down with the advent of discount brokers and Internet trading, but the costs have not gone away. And in addition to commissions, you must factor in tax consequences. When you sell a stock or a mutual fund and you realize a gain, you have to pay capital gains taxes on the profit for the year in which the profit was realized, unless you have offsetting losses on other transactions.

John Bogle, the legendary founder of the Vanguard Group of mutual funds and creator of the first index fund for individuals, has said that the best way to capture as much of the stock market's return as is possible is to buy and hold stocks and minimize the costs of investing. In this way, he says, investors can get 98 to 99 percent of the market's pretax annual return, after deducting costs.

So it pays to set your sights on the long term. And by long term, I don't mean two to three years, as some analysts define it. My definition of long term is at least 10 years. It's been my experience, and that of many others, that long-term investing is the best way to go for the average person—and that means most of us.

The market's history clearly shows the merits of long-term investing (see Figure 3-1). The S&P 500 index has racked up positive returns for any 10-year period in the past 50 years, which means that if you buy now and commit for a 10-year period, history says you will be a winner. Stocks over the long term also have beaten inflation by a wide margin. An analysis of 20-year holding periods between 1928 and the end of 2002 showed the S&P 500 average annual return was 11.9 percent, well above the inflation rate of 3.9 percent for the same period, while the average annual return for long-term government bonds was only 4.5 percent. The real (inflation-adjusted) rate for equities works out to 7.4 percent versus a real rate of 0.6 percent for bonds. And cash alternatives have done even worse than bonds over time. (See Figure 3-2.) As individuals discovered in the brutal 2000–2002 bear market, investment returns over the short term can be scary. In fact, in the worst periods of the latest bear market, many people literally couldn't face the bad numbers and didn't even bother to open their 401(k) or mutual fund statements.

As we've pointed out, the S&P 500 historically has averaged an 11.9 percent gain annually. Keep in mind that the return includes years of bear markets as well as bull markets. As Jeremy Siegel, a Wharton School professor and author of *Stocks for the Long Run*, observes, "Bear markets give stocks their superior rates of return. If there were no down markets, there would be no risk, and if there were no risk, there would be no 'risk premium'—the extra return that stocks earn over other safe assets, such as government bonds and certificates of deposit." He concludes, "It's because of the extraordinarily high returns stockholders receive if they buy at the tail end of a bear market that stocks beat all other financial assets, hands down."

In 20 recessions from 1902 to 1991, the S&P 500 rose an average of 10.3% three months after the end of the slowdown (see Figure 3-3). Twelve months after the end of each bear market since 1949, the S&P 500's average increase was 37 percent.

In order to benefit from the market's good returns, you must stay the course. Don't panic and sell out when the market is in a down-

FIGURE 3-1. Stock Market History Since 1928

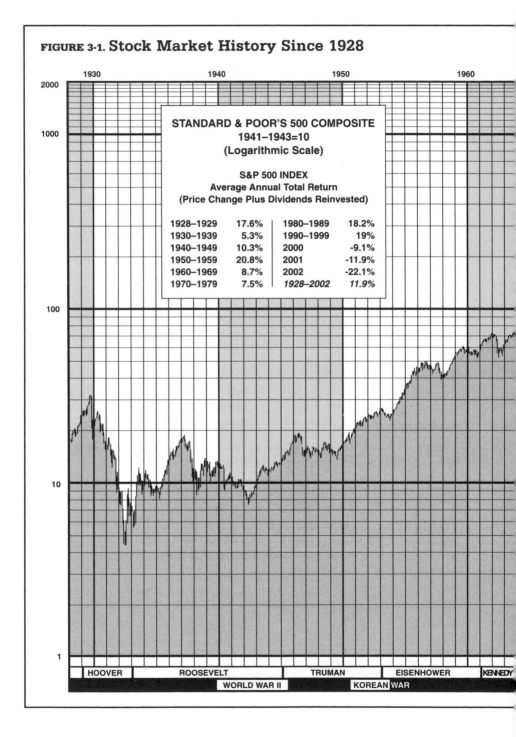

STANDARD & POOR'S 500 COMPOSITE
1941–1943=10
(Logarithmic Scale)

S&P 500 INDEX
Average Annual Total Return
(Price Change Plus Dividends Reinvested)

1928–1929	17.6%	1980–1989	18.2%
1930–1939	5.3%	1990–1999	19%
1940–1949	10.3%	2000	-9.1%
1950–1959	20.8%	2001	-11.9%
1960–1969	8.7%	2002	-22.1%
1970–1979	7.5%	1928–2002	11.9%

HOOVER   ROOSEVELT   TRUMAN   EISENHOWER   KENNEDY

WORLD WAR II   KOREAN WAR

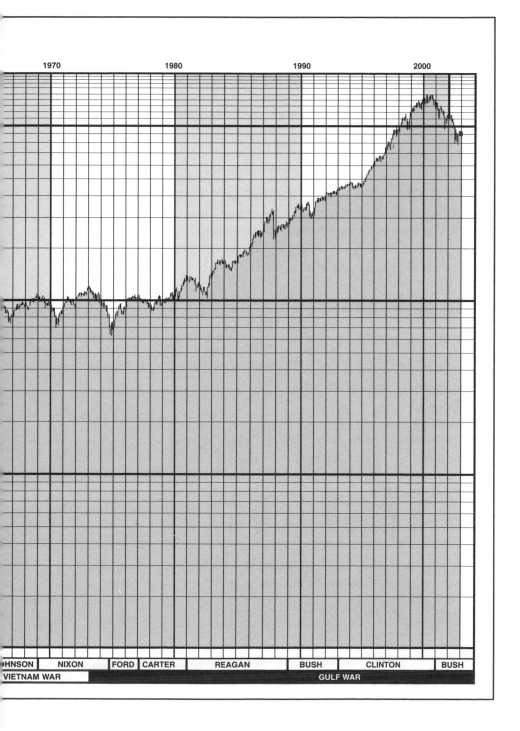

| 1970 | 1980 | 1990 | 2000 |

| HNSON | NIXON | FORD | CARTER | REAGAN | BUSH | CLINTON | BUSH |

VIETNAM WAR   GULF WAR

turn, and don't funnel more money than you were investing before into a market that's been rising for a long time. Again, discipline is the key. And the best way to stay focused is through dollar cost averaging (see Chapter 6). No matter what mode the market is in, keep investing a fixed dollar amount at regular intervals. You buy fewer shares when the market is high and more when it's low, thus smoothing the market's inevitable gyrations. The odds are in your favor that you'll come out way ahead when it's time to cash in.

Asset Allocation and the Long Run

A critical part of your long-term strategy is asset allocation. One only has to look at Enron to realize what can happen when one stock accounts for the lion's share of an employee's 401(k). And in the case of the technology bubble, one can see the dire consequences of concentrating in only one sector.

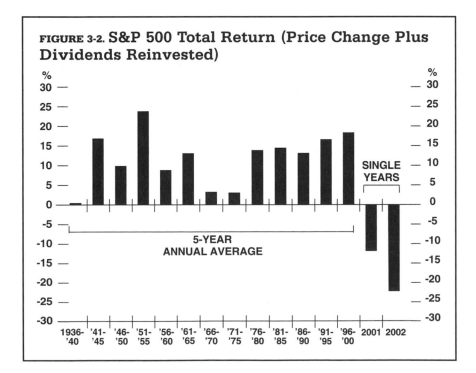

FIGURE 3-2. S&P 500 Total Return (Price Change Plus Dividends Reinvested)

Studies have shown that asset allocation, which is diversification with a twist, is the single most important factor in determining investment returns. It consists of dividing your investments among different asset categories, such as stocks (large, medium, and small capitalization, as well as stocks in different industries or sectors), bonds (government, corporate, and municipals—we'll go into these various bond types in Chapter 10), mutual funds, and cash (short-term certificates of deposit, money market funds, and short-term Treasuries. By having a diverse asset mix, you balance the potential risks and rewards of your investments. In other words (it's cliché time again), never keep all of your eggs in one basket.

With asset allocation, you divide your diversified assets by percentage. You have to decide how much of your portfolio you want to allocate to each asset class. In allocating a specific percentage of your money to stocks, bonds, or cash, for instance, you have to factor in the time you have available for investing and how much investment risk you're comfortable with. We'll scc some examples later in the chapter.

Allocation Can Determine an Investor's Success

History shows that few classes move in tandem. One year, large-cap stocks may generate the best returns, while in another it will

FIGURE 3-3. Recoveries in the Market 3 Months After the End of Recesssions

Recession	S&P 500 End of Recession to 3 Months After
9/02–8/04	17%
1/07–6/08	7%
1/10–1/12	5%
1/13–12/14	3%
8/18–3/19	13%
1/20–7/21	3%
5/23–7/24	1%
10/26–11/27	2%
8/29–3/33	43%
5/37–6/38	21%
2/45–10/45	18%
11/48–10/49	5%
7/53–5/54	7%
8/57–4/58	6%
4/60–2/61	8%
12/69–11/70	18%
11/73–3/75	7%
1/80–7/80	12%
7/81–11/82	8%
7/90–3/91	2%
Average 1902–2001	10.3%
Average 1948–2001	8.1%

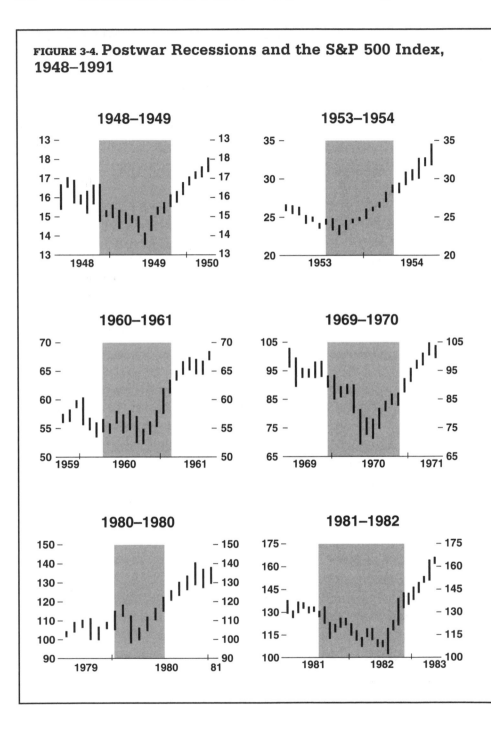

FIGURE 3-4. Postwar Recessions and the S&P 500 Index, 1948–1991

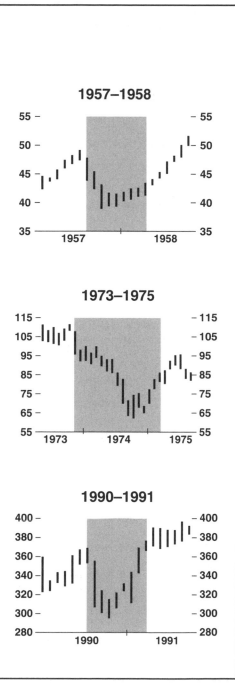

1957–1958

1973–1975

1990–1991

be small- and mid-cap stocks or government bonds. Also, some classes of assets are much more volatile than others. For example, technology stocks went from huge gains in 1999 to sickening losses in 2000–2001, while many bank stocks moved within a fairly narrow range. In 2000 and 2001, while large-cap stocks, as measured by the S&P 500, were down in both years, long-term corporate bonds returned 12.9 and 10.7 percent respectively.

It's best to include assorted types of investments that usually perform differently in various economic environments. When the economy is in a recession, for instance, defensive stocks are a good choice. These include companies in the consumer staples category (soft drinks, food, household and personal products, brewers, etc.), drugs, and utilities. The thinking is that even in a poor economy, people still need to buy the basics. Groups to avoid in an economic downturn, of course, are those companies whose fortunes are closely tied to general business conditions, otherwise known as cyclicals, such as steel, aluminum, chemicals, and paper.

Figure 3-4 on pages 30–31, shows that stock prices, which are one of the leading economic indicators, usually begin falling before the onset of a recession, hit bottom in the midst of the recession, then rise through the latter part of the recession and for a number of months afterward. Sometimes the market recovery starts early in the recession, sometimes rather late. But on average in the nine postwar recessions—the 10th, which began in March 2001 and officially ended in November 2001, was the exception—the S&P 500 index hit bottom six months after the recession started and five months before it ended.

Recessions

According to David Wyss, chief economist at Standard & Poor's, the definition of a recession is an art rather than a science. The National Bureau of Economic Research (NBER), the official arbiter, has a complicated definition that looks at a variety of economic indicators to measure the depth, diffusion, and duration of a downturn. The 3D picture of a recession is simplified for most observers by the rule of thumb that the economy is in recession if real (inflation-adjusted) gross national product (GDP) declines for two consecutive quarters. The rule doesn't always work, however—the 1960 recession had two negative quarters, but not in succession.

The end of a recession is equally difficult to define, though in practice it's usually clear. The outstanding exception was the 1980 and 1981–82 recessions. Economists are still arguing about whether that should count as one or two recessions, since the intervening recovery had only two consecutive quarters of growth.

From the market low during the nine official postwar recessions to six months after that point, the average gain in the S&P 500 was 38 percent. Twelve months after the market low, the average gain in the S&P 500 was 46 percent. In the 2001 recession, the S&P 500 hit bottom 19 months (in October 2002) after the recession started. In mid-July 2003, the NBER declared that the recession, which started in March 2001, bottomed in November 2001. The call was a controversial one, since there were 2 million unemployed at the time of the declaration.

Interest Rates

When interest rates are declining, as was the case in 2001, 2002, and the first half of 2003, government and corporate bonds are a good bet. Bond prices rise when interest rates are falling. However, the opposite is true when interest rates are on the ascendancy.

The uninitiated often jump into fixed-income investments—bonds and money market funds, which we'll discuss in Chapter 10—as a safe haven when the market is in a downtrend. That's okay, as long as interest rates don't climb. But once the Federal Reserve Board starts to hike up rates, bond prices often decline.

I remember a coworker in a state of shock after she had received a brokerage statement that showed a big drop in her bond mutual fund's net asset value. She said to me, "I thought bonds were safe, that's why I bought this fund!" Of course, if you buy an individual bond and hang on to it until it matures, you'll get your money back in full. But if you get into a bond fund or need the money before the individual bond matures and have to sell it, you may be out of luck. Again, fixed-income investments fluctuate with the interest rate trend.

Understanding Risk

In order to diversify properly, you need to take into account your investment time horizon: Will you need the money in 12 months, 12 years, or 20 years? You'll also need to be realistic about how much risk you're willing to assume. You can apply these two principles to different asset classes.

Understanding risk is basic in reaching your financial goals. All investments involve some risk that you may wind up losing money. Even if you keep your money buried in the backyard, there's the risk that someone may discover it, and if they don't, that your stash will be worth less over time because of the ravages of inflation: Your money will buy less.

Inflation is called the silent risk because of its quietly eroding nature. Over the last few years, it's been relatively mild, averaging about 3 percent annually. But even if it remains at this fairly tame level, a house that now costs $150,000 will cost $201,587 in 10 years, and maybe much more, depending on the real estate market. Ten years from now, a car you buy today for $18,000 will cost you $24,190. And you'll have to plunk down $47 in 10 years for a pair of jeans that costs $35 now. If inflation should double to 6 percent, the impact would be that much greater because of the compounding effect we discussed in the first chapter. See Figure 3-5.

Different types of investments carry different types of risks (see Figure 3-6). Stocks are influenced by various factors, such as the state of the economy, market psychology and interest rates, as well as by company specifics, including revenues, earnings, and manage-

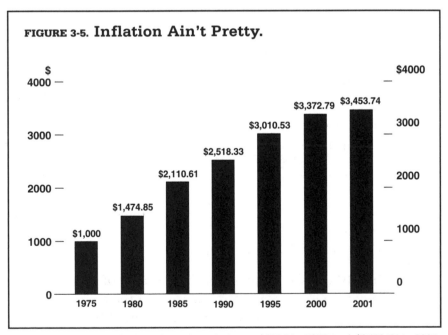

FIGURE 3-5. **Inflation Ain't Pretty.**

The same basket of goods and services that cost $1000 in 1975 cost $3453.74 in 2001, for an increase of 245%, based on the consumer price index.

FIGURE 3-6. **Asset Classes and Their Risks**

LOW RISK

These assets carry little risk of loss, though inflation can erode their value:

➤ Savings Accounts

➤ Money Market Accounts

➤ Treasury Bills and Notes

➤ Short-Term Certificates of Deposits (CDs)

MODERATE RISK

Bond prices fluctuate with interest rates. When rates are rising, you would lose money if you sold the bond before it matures:

➤ Investment-Grade Intermediate Bonds

➤ Investment-Grade Longer-Term Bonds

HIGHER RISK

Common stocks are the riskiest asset class, but they also have the best profit potential:

➤ Stocks

➤ Equity Mutual Funds

➤ High-Yield (Junk) Bonds

---

ment. Bonds are heavily influenced by interest rates and by the credit quality of the company.

In general, there are four types of risks:

➤ **MARKET RISK** is the likelihood that the value of a security will move in tandem with the overall market. If the stock market is declining, chances are your stocks and mutual funds will also drop. Or if bond prices are climbing, the value of your bonds will probably go up.

> **INTEREST RATE RISK** is associated with fixed-income investments and is the risk that the price of a bond or the price of a bond fund will fall with rising interest rates.

> **INFLATION RISK** is the risk that the value of your portfolio will be eroded by a decline in the purchasing power of your savings. Even though your investment may be posting gains, it may be losing value if it does not at least keep pace with the inflation rate.

> **CREDIT RISK,** which comes into play with bonds and bond funds, refers to the ability of the company that issues the bond to make the semiannual interest payments and to repay its debt as promised when the bond matures. Bonds and bond funds are given credit ratings by agencies such as Moody's and Standard & Poor's. Generally, the higher the rating, the lower the credit risk. High yield, or junk bonds, usually have the lowest ratings. (See Chapter 10 for more on bonds and credit ratings.)

You have to determine your tolerance for risk. As a way of finding out, consider Figure 3-7 and answer these questions:

> Is stability more important to you than higher returns?

> Would you be uncomfortable if your investment fell sharply over a short period of time?

> How much of your investment could you lose in one year and still stick to your long-term financial plan: 5 percent, 10 percent, 15 percent, or higher?

If you answered yes to the first two questions, you obviously should concentrate on more conservative investments, such as short-term bonds and money market funds. (You'll find a more comprehensive test at the end of this chapter.)

If your goal is above-average returns, you have to accept higher risk. You must balance the amount of risk you're willing to take with the amount of reward you're looking for. Even though you have a relatively low risk tolerance, you can diversify into riskier investments if you keep the overall risk of your investments (a.k.a. your portfolio) on the low side.

An example of an aggressive (more risk-oriented) portfolio of someone who has a 20-year investment time horizon may be the following: 50 percent large-cap stocks, 10 percent mid-cap stocks, 10 percent small-cap stocks, 15 percent international stocks, and 15 percent bonds. This is considered aggressive because of the small fixed-income exposure; 85 percent stocks puts you more at risk.

For an investor who'll need to cash out in five to 10 years, this mix would be appropriate: 40 percent large-cap stocks, 10 percent medium-cap, 5 percent small-cap, 5 percent international, 35 percent bonds, 5 percent money market funds. Here the allocation is less risky because the mix is 40 percent fixed to 60 percent stocks.

Those more conservatively inclined who need the money within five to 10 years could consider 60 percent bonds, 10 percent money

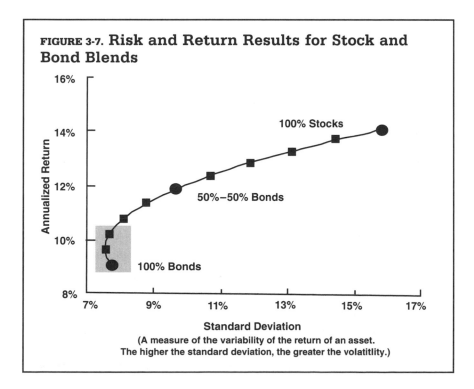

FIGURE 3-7. **Risk and Return Results for Stock and Bond Blends**

Annualized Return

100% Stocks

50%–50% Bonds

100% Bonds

Standard Deviation
(A measure of the variability of the return of an asset.
The higher the standard deviation, the greater the volatitlity.)

market funds, and the rest equally divided among large-, medium-, and small-cap stocks, as well as international issues.

If you don't have much money to invest, say less than $50,000, it's impossible to diversify with individual stocks. In that case, the best course is via mutual funds. The total market funds offered by T. Rowe Price and Vanguard (see the Appendix) will give you an excellent mix of international stocks and large-, small-, and medium-cap stocks. Both funds are no load, tax efficient, and have low expense ratios, which we'll discuss in Chapter 7.

A caveat: Diversification is important. But you want to avoid what Warren Buffett calls "di-worse-ification." You don't need to own more than 15 or 20 stocks. If you go much above that number, you'll find it difficult to keep up with what's happening with your investment brood and dilute your chances of an above-average return.

According to Ibbotson Associates, here's how various portfolios have performed, on average, annually from 1926 through 2002:

➤ An aggressive portfolio of 75 percent stocks, 20 percent bonds, and 5 percent money market funds returned 9.6 percent.

➤ A moderate portfolio of 60 percent stocks, 30 percent bonds, and 10 percent money market funds returned 8.8 percent.

➤ A conservative portfolio of 40 percent stocks, 45 percent bonds, and 15 percent money market funds returned 7.7 percent.

Managing Your Investments

You should review your investment program regularly. Take a close look at least once a year to make sure your asset mix is continuing to meet your investment objectives, risk tolerance, and time horizon.

If you find your allocation has changed because one asset class has been a big winner or a big loser, you should rebalance your portfolio. If, for example, you had 50 percent of your portfolio in large-cap stocks, and the group does so well that it now represents 65 percent of the total worth of your portfolio, you should rebalance. Sell some of your large-caps and spread the money among your asset classes that have not done as well.

It's tough to sell your winners and buy your losers, and it may even sound like bad advice. But in the long run it's worth it. If more investors had rebalanced during the tech bubble, selling their expensive stocks and putting the proceeds into more conservatively valued issues and a money market fund or short-term bond fund, they would have saved a bundle on anti-depressants. (See Chapter 8 for more on when to sell.)

Risk Tolerance Test

The source of this test to measure your investment time horizon and risk tolerance is the Securities Industry Association. Score 1 point for (a) answers, 2 points for (b) answers, 3 points for (c) answers, and 4 points for (d) answers. An evaluation of the scores follows the test.

1. I plan on using the money I'm investing: (a) within six months, (b) within three years, (c) between three and six years, (d) no sooner than seven years from now.

2. Excluding my home, my investments make up the following share of my assets: (a) more than 75 percent, (b) 50 percent or more but less than 75 percent, (c) 25 percent or more but less than 50 percent, (d) less than 25 percent.

3. I expect my future income to: (a) decrease, (b) remain the same or grow slowly, (c) grow faster than the inflation rate, (d) grow quickly.

4. I have emergency savings: (a) no, (b) yes, but much less than I'd like to have, (c) yes, but somewhat less than I'd like to have, (d) yes.

5. I would risk the following percentage of my investments in exchange for the same probability of doubling my money: (a) zero, (b) 50 percent, (c) 25 percent, (d), 10 percent.

6. I have invested in stocks and mutual funds: (a) no, and I don't wish to, (b) yes, but I was uneasy about it, (c) no, but I look forward to it, (d) yes, and I was comfortable with it.

7. My most important investment goal is to: (a) preserve my original investment, (b) receive some growth and provide income, (c) grow faster than inflation but still provide some income, (d) grow as fast as possible. Income is not important today.

Assessment: If your total score is 25 points or higher, you are an aggressive investor; between 20 and 24 points, your risk tolerance is above average; between 15 and 19 points, you're a moderate investor (one who is willing to accept some risk in exchange for a potential higher rate of return). If you scored fewer than 15 points, you are a conservative investor; fewer than 10 points, you're an ultra-conservative investor.

Points To Remember

➤ Many studies (and personal experience) have shown that long-term investors beat short-termers hands down. A "buy and bye-bye" approach rarely works. Stay invested in sound stocks and mutual funds even in down markets. Bull markets last much longer than bear markets, and gains on the upside far outweigh losses on the downside.

➤ Long-term investors enjoy the benefits of compounding, as well as lower taxes and commissions.

➤ In order to benefit from the market's historical 11.9 percent annual average rate of return, you must stay the course. Don't panic and sell out when the market is spiraling downward, and don't pour more money than you had been investing into a market that's been climbing for a long time.

➤ Asset allocation is the single most important factor in meeting your investment objectives, since the different asset classes don't all perform the same in any given period. As a general rule, put as much into equities as your investment time horizon and risk tolerance can best accommodate.

➤ Diversify among large-, medium-, and small-cap stocks, as well as bonds, money market funds, and international stocks.

➤ Think about both risk and return before you invest. The test on pages 39–40 will help you determine the level of risk you are willing to take.

➤ If you don't have much money to invest, the best way to diversify is through a total market fund. Vanguard and T. Rowe Price are tops.

➤ You don't need to buy more than 15 or 20 stocks. Otherwise, you have what Warren Buffett calls "di-worse-ification."

➤ At least once a year, check to see if your portfolio needs rebalancing. Often, one asset class turns in a strong performance, which puts your allocation out of whack. Also rebalance if your personal situation changes, such as marriage, divorce, or retirement.

CHAPTER 4

The Third Key: Buy What You Know and Don't Get Bubble-Wrapped

Understand a company's business. Investment advisers often tell those just starting to dip their toes into the market to buy stocks of companies they know and trust. In view of the many recent corporate scandals, that is sound advice —especially the trust part.

Two prominent money managers who are far from novices—Peter Lynch and Warren Buffett—have made a lot of money for themselves and their investors by sticking to companies they know and understand. Lynch managed the Fidelity Magellan Fund from 1977 to 1990. One of the best performing mutual funds during that period, Magellan outperformed the S&P 500 index by a compound annual rate of more than 10 percent. Lynch is now vice chairman of Fidelity Management & Research, the investment arm of Fidelity.

Warren Buffett, known as the "Sage of Omaha," is the power behind Berkshire Hathaway. That company owns insurers GEICO and General Re and has large holdings in firms that make everyday products such as Gillette, Coca-Cola, carpet maker Shaw Industries, and paint manufacturer Benjamin Moore. Its stock has returned 6.1 percent over the five-year period ended January 31, 2003, compared to the loss of 1.3 percent for the S&P 500.

During the high-tech bubble, Buffett was roundly criticized for missing the boat. But despite the brickbats, he stuck to his guns and didn't buy stocks of companies he didn't understand. And even if he did know what the tech companies were all about, he wouldn't buy the stocks because of their outrageous price-earnings multiples (P/E is the price of the stock divided by per-share profits; more on this later in the chapter). In many cases, in spite of their inflated stock prices, the companies had no earnings whatsoever. In the late 1990s one research director told me that Buffett was a dinosaur. He said that Buffett's time had come and was long gone. Technology was the way to riches, and poor old Warren was locked in the horse and buggy days.

Guess which one not only survived but thrived when the tech bubble burst?

Peter Lynch also says he has to thoroughly understand a company's business before he will commit to it. He believes you can make good investments by observing everyday life. When you go shopping, for example, and you're impressed by the merchandise and the reasonable prices a store offers and the big crowds the retailer is attracting, that could be a green light for more research on the company.

That guideline has worked for me. Several years ago, when a Wal-Mart store opened in my area, I was taken with the wide variety of merchandise, very competitive prices, and good service. The stock was depressed at the time, so, after doing some homework, I decided the shares were a good value. Since then, the stock has more than doubled.

Over the longer term, Lynch believes there is a strong correlation between a company's success and the success of the stock. Warren Buffett believes similarly. Buffett is not concerned with fluctuations in the stock market or the economy. He looks for businesses that are simple, understandable, have a successful operating history, and favorable long-term prospects.

When you buy stock in a company you know and trust, whenever you buy its products or use its service, you help increase that company's revenues and profits, and ultimately the stock price.

Investing in stocks of companies you're comfortable with is also an excellent way to get children involved in the stock market. You can buy shares via a discount broker or direct purchase plans in the name of your child, grandchild, godchild, niece, or nephew. Get started with a company a child is likely to connect with, such as Walt Disney, McDonald's, Coca-Cola, Toys 'R' Us, or Wrigley. When the statements and annual reports arrive, you could go over them with him or her. It's a fun learning experience that gets the novice investor interested in the stock market and the economy.

It cannot be emphasized enough that you shouldn't underestimate your stock-picking talents. You don't need an MBA or a CFA (chartered financial analyst) after your name to make money in the stock market. As Warren Buffett has said, "You don't need to be a rocket scientist. Investing is not a game where the guy with the 160 IQ beats the guy with the 130 IQ."

The next time you go to the mall or supermarket or do business with a company, think in terms of investment. Trust your instincts, do your homework, and you could wind up with some big winners right in your own backyard.

Doing the Homework

Your local library is a good place to start. Most libraries carry *The Value Line Investment Survey*, a weekly publication providing data on 1700 stocks. Standard & Poor's also publishes many useful products you can probably find in your library. These include *The Outlook*, a weekly investment advisory newsletter; *Stock Guide*, which contains key data on more than 11,000 common stocks, preferred stocks, and mutual funds; *Industry Surveys*, which provides in-depth analyses of 53 different industries; and *Stock Reports*, which covers about 5000 companies.

There are also many useful websites. Some of the better ones are:

➤ **http://finance.yahoo.com** is a provider of stock quotes, charts, and fundamental and technical research data

- ➤ **www.dailystocks.com** is organized into various categories, each with many links to other websites

- ➤ **www.standardandpoors.com** provides valuable data, including the Standard & Poor's benchmark indexes

- ➤ **www.businessweek.com/investor** is a good site for general business and stock market overviews

- ➤ **www.cbsmarketwatch.com** has commentary and analysis by staff writers and outside contributors

- ➤ **www.moneycentral.msn.com** provides good market commentary and boasts first-rate portfolio-tracking software

If you do your homework, chances are you won't wind up following the herd, which has proved to be a money-losing proposition over the years. Often, the herd is simply following a trend that is profitable for a few investors in the short term, but a disaster for most over the longer haul.

Don't Get Caught Up in Fashions

Let's take a look at some of the past fads, or "bubbles," as they're called on Wall Street.

The most recent bubble, which we mentioned earlier, was the high-tech, dot-com craze of the late 1990s. Shares of semiconductor companies, computer networking firms, PC makers, and any company with a dot-com in its name skyrocketed, regardless of the business fundamentals or the stock's valuation. The S&P technology index soared 75 percent in 1999, followed by a 40 percent drop in 2000. In 2001, the S&P information technology index fell 36 percent, with subindexes office electronics, telecom equipment, and computer storage and peripherals plummeting 79, 63, and 74 percent respectively.

Internet stocks witnessed the most dramatic price increases. Amazon.com and Yahoo soared tenfold in a year. TheStreet.com Internet index ballooned 149 percent from December 1998 to April

1999—that's less than five months. The Internet, by any measure, was one of the fastest growing commercial phenomena ever witnessed. The problem, though, was that few of the companies made any money. It was all pie in the sky. But lack of earnings—which analysts said weren't relevant—didn't stop investors from bidding up the group to ridiculous heights.

The tech bubble wasn't the only fad to win the hearts and minds of investors. As Federal Reserve Chairman Alan Greenspan observed, "Regrettably, history is strewn with visions of such 'new eras,' which in the end have proven to be a mirage."

In the 1980s, biotech and personal computer (PC) stocks were the Wall Street darlings. There were at least 500 biotech companies (75 percent privately held), and their products were expected to cure every sickness imaginable. Analysts were forecasting earnings that would explode a few years down the road. But what exploded were the stocks themselves. From the mid- to the late 1980s, most biotech issues lost at least 75 percent of their market value.

As for PCs, hundreds of companies began manufacturing them after IBM introduced its PC in 1981. Only a few years later, however, many of the firms, such as Commodore and Eagle Computer, threw in the towel after a sea of red ink washed over them. And those stocks that survived did poorly for many years.

In the 1970s, the "Nifty Fifty" was in vogue. The idea was, if you bought 50 of the largest-capitalization, blue-chip stocks, you were all set. Members of the Nifty Fifty at the time, which included such stellar names as IBM, Eastman Kodak, Xerox, Walt Disney, Polaroid, Avon Products, and McDonald's, were considered "one-decision" stocks. The investor made a decision to buy these stocks once, and then he or she never had to worry about the future.

The Nifty Fifty companies were fundamentally strong, unlike many of the stocks in other crazes. The problem was, the issues were bid up to unrealistic price levels. Price-earnings multiples of 80 or 90 were common. And, of course, as always happens when a stock is overpriced, one by one the Nifty Fifty collapsed. The group then became bargain-priced, and if you had bought the stocks at the lows, you would have done very well for yourself in the 1980s and 1990s.

Conglomerate was the magic word in the 1960s. Investors flocked to stocks of companies that acquired many different types of businesses, such as Litton Industries and LTV. The idea was that acquisitions, even those unrelated to a company's core business, could result in steadily increasing earnings, since a growth company could use its high price-earnings multiple stock to buy the shares of another company that carried a much lower multiple. This would theoretically boost earnings and thus the price of the acquirer.

The conglomeration worked—for a while. The party ended when Litton and others started to report disappointing earnings after years of steadily rising profits. Then, the stocks lost about half of their value. Today, there are not that many companies with scores of unrelated businesses. General Electric, Tyco International, and Textron are some of the current conglomerate-type companies, and their stock prices have been far from gangbusters in recent years. In fact, academic studies indicate that more than two-thirds of all acquisitions are not successful.

One of the original and perhaps the best known bubbles was the tulip mania that seized the Dutch in the 17th century. Tulips were first imported into Western Europe from Turkey in the mid-1500s. The beautiful, exotic flowers became very popular, and the demand, especially for rare varieties, couldn't keep up with the supply. As a result, prices soared, and there was a frenzy of speculation. Holland, which was the biggest producer of the bulbs, became the Nasdaq of its time. Some of the rarer bulbs sold for hundreds of dollars, a fortune in those days; one particular beauty went for $20,000. People mortgaged their homes and businesses to buy the bulbs.

The Dutch government warned about the speculative fervor, but, as with all bubbles, warnings and logic were ignored. Finally, in 1637, the government said that tulips were products, not investments, and they had to be bought and sold on that basis. Furthermore, the banks could no longer accept the flowers as collateral for loans. The crash that occurred shortly afterward bankrupted thousands of Dutch citizens and practically cleaned out the national treasury as tax revenues sank.

The moral of these bubble tales: If one market sector is hot, hot, hot for some time, don't jump in. Even though it may not be too late to make money, you probably won't know when to bail out. Stick to investing in companies you know and trust, and where the stock valuation is reasonable.

In the next chapter, we'll look at ways to help you determine if a stock is overpriced.

Points To Remember

➤ In buying individual stocks, it's best to invest in reasonably valued stocks of companies you know and trust; companies you feel have a sustainable competitive advantage over their peers.

➤ Two of the most successful investors ever—Warren Buffett and Peter Lynch—follow the adage that familiarity can breed capital gains.

➤ Do your homework. Use your local library to access reports and data published by Value Line and Standard & Poor's. Try to read such first-rate financial newspapers like the *Wall Street Journal* and *Investor's Business Daily*. Many different websites also have useful information on investing.

➤ Remember the various investment bubbles over the years. More will crop up periodically. But don't be tempted to join the party. Don't get "bubble-wrapped." Don't chase performance. Don't pick last year's winners. Have a clear buy and sell strategy.

CHAPTER 5

To Buy or Not to Buy

O ne of the basic rules of investing is not to pay too much for a stock. To their regret, as we've seen, many people tossed that rule out the window during the roaring bull market of the late 1990s.

How to Tell If a Stock Is Overvalued

You can use various measures to help determine the value of a stock. These include:

> ➤ Price-to-earnings ratio
>
> ➤ Price-to-sales ratio
>
> ➤ Price-to-cash-flow ratio

In other words, the stock price relative to earnings, sales, and cash flow.

Price-to-Earnings Ratio

The most popular indicator is the P/E, which is shorthand for the ratio of a company's share price to its per-share earnings. A P/E of 15, for example, indicates that investors are willing to pay $15 for every dollar of yearly earnings the company generates.

To calculate the P/E, divide the current stock price of a company by its earnings per share. The P/E is also referred to as the *multiple*,

[51]

because it shows how much investors are willing to pay for each dollar of earnings. For example, if a stock sells at $30 and the company earned $2 a share, then the P/E is 15 (30 divided by 2). You can use either trailing earnings (over the past 12 months), or analysts' estimates of current-year earnings. Professionals usually refer to estimated earnings.

But the P/E by itself is not enough to assess a stock. You also have to compare the stock's P/E to its historical P/E, as well as to the P/E of its peers and to the P/E of a market benchmark, such as the S&P 500 index. It's also a good idea to compare the P/E to the projected three- or five-year per-share earnings growth rate, although often this so-called PEG rate (P/E to expected growth) can be pie-in-the-sky, since it's difficult enough to estimate earnings even one year ahead.

Price-to-Sales Ratio

In view of the earnings manipulations seen in recent years, the price-to-sales ratio has become increasingly valuable as an analytical tool. Revenues, or sales, can't be "massaged" as profits often are. Share buy-backs, whereby a company will repurchase its own shares, or downsizing, can make per-share earnings look strong while a company's basic business is sluggish.

As the name implies, the price-to-sales ratio is the stock's price divided by the company's sales or revenues. Since the sales number is not usually expressed as a per-share figure, it's easier to divide a stock's total market value—price times number of shares outstanding—by the total sales for the past 12 months. Generally, if a stock is trading at a price-to-sales ratio of 1.0, it may be a good buy. For example, if Ajax has sales of $1 billion and a market value of $900 million, the price to sales ratio is 0.9, which means you can buy a dollar of its sales for only 90 cents.

In *What Works on Wall Street*, James O'Shaughnessy notes that stocks with low price-to-sales ratios outperformed stocks with low price-to-earnings ratios. He also discovered that price-to-sales ratios worked best for large-cap stocks. In contrast, the ratio doesn't work well for service companies, such as financial institutions, which don't have traditional sales.

As with the price-to-earnings ratio, you should compare a stock's price-to-sales ratio to that of its peers and to its historical ratio.

Price-to-Cash-Flow Ratio

This ratio is another reliable financial indicator. A company's cash flow—its net income plus depreciation minus working capital needs—shows how much flexibility management may have when it comes to reinvesting in the business, repurchasing stock, paying down debt, boosting dividends, and making acquisitions: measures that might increase shareholder value.

Again, the ratio—calculated by dividing the share price by cash flow—should be compared with the company's historical ratio, as well as those of it competitors and the overall market's price-to-cash-flow ratios.

Studying the Balance Sheet

In addition to researching price-to-earnings ratios, price-to-sales ratios, and price-to-cash-flow ratios, you should examine a company's balance sheet. This is a statement of the total assets and liabilities of a company at a particular time, usually the last date of an accounting period. One side of the balance sheet adds up assets, which lists them from the most liquid (cash) to the least liquid (plant and equipment). The other side lists liabilities in the order of how soon they have to be paid. Assets must equal liabilities plus shareholders' equity (total assets minus total liabilities). Shareholders' equity is also called *owner's equity* or *net worth* or *net assets*.

Using a company's balance sheet, you can compare current assets (assets that can be converted to cash in less than a year) and current liabilities (money owned that is due within a year) to assess liquidity. You can compare debt to shareholders' equity to see how *leveraged* the company is; that is, how much debt it owes.

For conservative investors, a strong balance sheet is a must. If a company has little or no debt, it tends to be conservatively managed. Also, (1) if a company's cash position is greater than its long-term debt, and (2) its current assets—or assets that can be converted to cash in less than a year—are greater than its current liabilities plus its long-term debt, then it is financially sound and should be able to weather any economic storms.

Companies publish their balance sheets in their reports, and you can also find them in Standard & Poor's Stock Reports, as well as in Value Line's service.

Discounted Cash Flow Analysis

Securities analysts widely use discounted flow analysis, or DCF, to determine a stock's current value according to the company's estimated future cash flow.

Here's how it breaks down: A company's forecasted free *cash flow*—operating profit plus *depreciation* plus *amortization* of *goodwill* minus capital expenditures minus cash taxes minus change in *working capital*—is discounted to a present value using the company's weighted average costs of capital.

To better understand this: *Cash flow* is a company's operating income less expenses, taxes, and changes in net working capital and investments; or a measure of profitability after all expenses and reinvestments. *Depreciation* is an expense recorded to reduce the value of a long-term tangible asset, such as equipment; it's a noncash expense, so it increases free cash flow while reducing the amount of a company's reported earnings. *Amortization* is the paying off of debt in regular installments over a period of time. *Goodwill* is the excess of the purchase price over the fair market value of an asset (usually an acquired company). And *working capital* is current assets minus current liabilities.

Discounted cash flow analysis is often used to come up with a target price for a stock. Standard & Poor's equity analysts use DCF analysis to calculate the fair value—or target—prices for the stocks they follow. Some of these target prices are published in S&P's weekly investment advisory newsletter, *The Outlook*.

Of course, as with other valuation tools, discounted cash flow analysis is far from a science. A lot depends on guesswork. Small changes in the variables that are used to calculate DCF can result in large changes in the estimated value of a stock. A meaningful valuation depends on one's ability to make solid cash-flow projections, and with uncertainty a fact of corporate life, what appears solid can in fact be on the mushy side.

DCF, though, is worth a look. But don't rely on it solely in making a decision on whether to buy a stock.

Technical Analysis

Our discussion of price-to-earnings ratios, price-to-sales ratios, price-to-cash-flow ratio, the balance sheet, and discounted cash flow analysis are part of *fundamental analysis*, which involves examining the company's financials and operations. These financials and operations take in sales, earnings, growth potential, assets, debt, management, and competition. Fundamental analysis considers only those variables that are directly related to the company, rather than the overall state of the market.

Technical analysis is a whole 'nother ball game. It's the study of the internal behavior of financial markets in order to measure the degree of demand or supply for the underlying securities, which can help investors detect patterns that anticipate or confirm market shifts, and to better time their buy and sell decisions.

Technicians follow different indicators. Some study price trends. Others focus on momentum or the strength of the market's advance or decline. Still others measure investor expectations or sentiment. Another group tracks monetary or economic trends, such as interest rates. But no single indicator tells the entire story. Combining fundamental and technical analysis brings a more balanced approach to the investment decision-making process.

The basic tools of the technician are charts, and most charts tracing markets are based on indexes and contain three elements: price, volume, and a moving average. Data are usually daily or weekly. Volume, usually depicted by vertical lines at the bottom of the chart, shows daily or weekly trading activity. A moving average of the price, which shows the underlying trend of an index, is calculated over a specific time period: 10 weeks (50 days) or 40 weeks (200 days) are common. The longer the period of time, the greater its significance in identifying a trend.

Technicians look at the interrelationship of the price and moving average to help determine trend changes. For example, when the price crosses above the moving average and the moving average turns up, the trend has become positive. When the price crosses below the moving average and the moving average turns down, the trend has become negative. In a situation in which the moving average has been relatively flat and the price has tended to oscillate above and below it, the index has been confined to what is known as a *trading range*.

Three Basic Market Indicators

Three categories of technical gauges are used to interpret what the market is trying to tell us: trend-following, momentum, and sentiment. Trend-following data illustrate or confirm whether prices are moving up or down. Momentum statistics measure the rate of change or intensity of an advance or decline. And sentiment measures provide insights into the expectations of specific groups of investors, such as stock options traders, small investors, or corporate insiders.

Five Widely Followed Technical Indicators

S&P 500 INDEX AND 40-WEEK MOVING AVERAGE (the average price over 40 weeks) shows the index's long-term underlying trend. When the S&P 500 (or any other index) is above its moving average, the trend is up; when below, its trend is down. The S&P 500 decisively broke below its 40-week moving average in October 2000, heralding the start of a downtrend. See Figure 5-1.

S&P 500 VERSUS NYSE DAILY ADVANCE-DECLINE LINE, a measure of market breadth, calculates the cumulative difference between daily advancing and declining stocks on the New York Stock Exchange (NYSE). From December 2000 through April 2002, the

NYSE A-D line trended upward. This is known as a "stealth" bull market, in which small- and mid-capitalization issues typically do well, while large-cap stocks languish. See Figure 5-2 on page 58.

NET NEW 52-WEEK HIGHS (HIGHS MINUS LOWS) OF INDIVIDUAL STOCKS ON A WEEKLY BASIS is an indicator of market participation. Until March 2002, the number of net new 52-week highs was trending upward. In other words, more and more stocks were participating in the advance that began in September 2001. By June 2002, however, net new lows substantially exceeded highs, indicating a shift in leadership from the upside to the downside. In late July 2002 this measure reached an extremely low level normally associated with market troughs. See Figure 5-3 on page 59.

YEAR-TO-YEAR CHANGE IN THE LEHMAN BROTHERS LONG-TERM U.S. TREASURY BOND INDEX. When weekly U.S. Treasury bond prices, as measured by this index, are up on a year-to-year basis, long-term interest rates have been trending lower, reflecting or suggesting an easy Federal Reserve monetary policy and lower short-term rates. Conversely, if Treasury bond prices are down and long rates have been trending higher, tighter Fed policy and rising short-term rates are likely. A longstanding positive year-to-year change in U.S. Treasuries means that the Fed has the flexibility to maintain easy money, or keep short-term interest rates low, for the foreseeable future. Low or declining interest rates are generally bullish for stocks because they make it easier for businesses and the economy to grow, and they make fixed-income investments a less appealing alternative to stocks.

CBOE OPTIONS VOLATILITY INDEX. A contrary indicator, the VIX gauges the sentiment of index options traders. Low readings, which indicate complacency, are bearish for the stock market; but high levels, which reveal fear, are bullish. The index spiked in the wake of the September 11 terrorist attack, but gave way to low readings from March to June 2002. See Figure 5-4 on page 59.

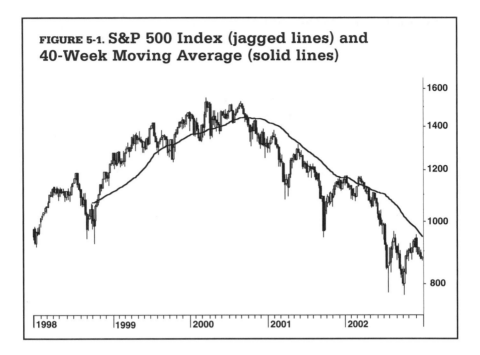

FIGURE 5-1. S&P 500 Index (jagged lines) and 40-Week Moving Average (solid lines)

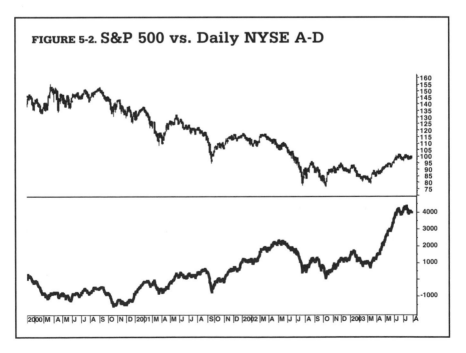

FIGURE 5-2. S&P 500 vs. Daily NYSE A-D

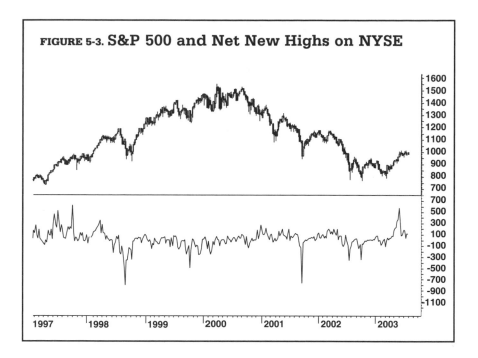

FIGURE 5-3. S&P 500 and Net New Highs on NYSE

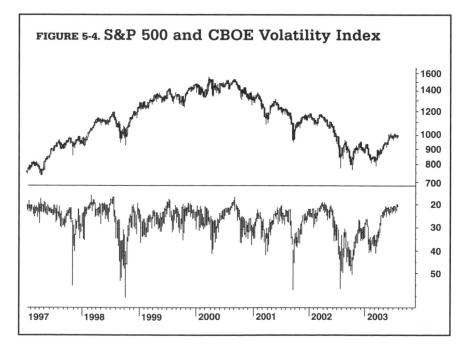

FIGURE 5-4. S&P 500 and CBOE Volatility Index

How to Use Market Indicators

Fundamental analysis is often premature in calling market tops and bottoms, since the market can become increasingly overvalued or undervalued in the short run before a trend has fully run its course. On the other hand, technical analysis often is late in signaling market turns, as chart patterns are only apparent in hindsight. Their combination, therefore, represents a more balanced approach to the investment decision-making process.

Let's say, for example, that the stock market has declined and a number of stocks that you believe are undervalued have fallen as well. You want to use this sell-off as a buying opportunity, but a look at the latest market indicators shows that the overall outlook has turned decidedly negative. Because there's a possibility that the market could go much lower, you may wish to defer your purchase until conditions stabilize.

Conversely, let's say the market has advanced dramatically and you've come to the conclusion that some of your stocks are fundamentally overvalued. However, an examination of market technical measures reveals that the major indexes are in well-defined uptrends with few signs of topping out and an absence of speculative excesses. In this case, the investor might be better off delaying a sell decision until the indexes begin to move sideways.

Points to Remember

➤ In determining if a stock is a good value, research its price-to-earnings ratio and its price-to-sales ratio relative to its historical ratios and to those of the company's peers. Also, look into the fair value price of a stock, based on its discounted cash flow.

➤ Technical analysis is also useful, but is more of an art than a science. Conclusions are only as good as the technician, who makes subjective evaluations based on knowledge and experience.

➤ No single indicator, technical or fundamental, is always correct in forecasting the market. Thus, the direction of a preponderance of technical indicators should be considered in coming to any conclusion.

➤ Divergences between indexes and broader-based measures, such as the advance-decline line, are usually resolved in favor of the direction of the broader based one.

➤ Important turning points are usually reached at extremes. In some cases, however, the trend can change without conditions becoming quite as extreme as they did previously. In other situations, a trend reversal may not occur until the atmosphere becomes more highly charged than it's ever been.

➤ Generally, old support levels (floors) once violated become new resistance (ceilings), whereas old resistance levels (ceilings) once broken become new support (floors).

CHAPTER 6

The Fourth Key: Dollar Cost Averaging— A Tried and True Method

Someone once asked the astute financier J. P. Morgan what the stock market would do on a particular day. His classic response: "It will fluctuate!"

That's about the only safe prediction one can make when it comes to forecasting the market. As we've stressed, over the longer run stock returns have handily beaten other investments, including bonds, precious metals, and real estate. But the market does indeed fluctuate, and over the past few years it has had some wild swings, both on the upside and downside.

An excellent way to make the inevitable market gyrations work for you is through dollar cost averaging. This entails investing equal amounts of money in a stock or mutual fund at regular intervals. It's a simple concept, but the secret of successful investing, as with life in general, is to keep it simple.

Some supposedly more sophisticated financial advisers may scoff at dollar cost averaging because it's too easy. And brokers prefer that you invest lump sums—so they can realize fatter commissions. But as one who has adhered to the practice for many years, I can assert that dollar cost averaging has proved a highly successful investment strategy for me, as it will for you.

A Faithful Commitment

The key is to select appropriate investments and *to faithfully make the periodic dollar commitments*. You must continue to invest, whether the market is soaring, plunging, or moving sideways, and no matter what the "experts" are saying.

It's amazing, by the way, how many people take as gospel truth the nonsense that's often spouted on financial TV programs and in the financial press. Nobody knows what the market is going to do from day to day, week to week, or month to month. But the average Joe thinks that because a glib, sharp-looking guy or gal is being interviewed on CNBC or is quoted in the press, they must know what they're talking about. *News flash!* More often than not it's just noise.

Back to dollar cost averaging: It can't be stressed enough that in order to make it work, you've got to be fully committed to it. That way you avoid emotional pitfalls and you don't get sandbagged by the "news du jour." I once had a discussion with a well-regarded economist about the subject. The market at the time was deep in bear territory. I told him that despite the gloom, I continued to invest via dollar cost averaging. The economist said that he too was a firm believer in that investment method, but he didn't think it wise to dollar cost average then because the market was acting so poorly.

Talk about missing the boat! Someone observed that being a weatherman or an economist is a great job because if you're wrong, you still get paid. The whole rationale behind dollar cost averaging is to stay in the market at all times. If you're investing in sound companies, you should be happy when stocks are sinking because your money will buy more shares with each purchase.

The best way to dollar cost average is to have money automatically taken out of your checking or savings account each month. Most mutual funds have this feature, as well as direct purchase plans and dividend reinvestment plans. This automatic approach ensures that you'll buy more shares when the price of your stock or mutual fund is low and fewer shares when the price is high. As a result, the average amount you pay for each share—the average cost per share—will be lower than the average price per share. In truth, investing a large amount of money at the right time can be more profitable than dollar cost averaging, but how many investors know exactly when the right time presents itself?

Of course, sometimes it happens that the stock or fund in which you're dollar cost averaging doesn't work out. If you're in an investment that has fallen more than the S&P 500 index over several months, then you have to decide whether to sell and get into another security. Again, do your homework. If the fundamentals have not changed, continue to dollar cost average, since you'll be getting a lot more shares for your money. But if there's been some dramatic change—such as a large acquisition that proves to be a clinker, for instance, or a pattern of restating earnings—then it's time to pull the plug.

How It Works

Here's an example of how dollar cost averaging plays out. Let's say every month you buy $200 worth of a blue-chip stock directly from the company:

> ➤ The first month, the stock trades for $60 a share. Your $200 buys 3.3 shares. Yes, 3.3 shares. (One of the big pluses in buying from most mutual funds or via direct purchase plans or dividend reinvestment plans is that you can buy fractional shares.)

> ➤ The next month, the stock sells for $50 a share. Your $200 investment now buys four shares.

> ➤ The third month, the stock rises to $65, and your $200 investment buys 3.1 shares.

> ➤ The fourth month, the stock slips back to the $60 level, and your $200 buys 3.3 shares again.

At the end of four months, you've invested $800 to purchase 13.7 shares at an average price of $58.39, which is lower than the $60 price it traded at four months earlier. You have a profit of $1.61 a share because when the stock dropped, you bought more shares.

FIGURE 6-1. Dollar Cost Averaging

FLUCTUATING MARKET

Amounts Invested	Share Price	Shares Acquired
$100	$10	10
100	10	20
100	5	10
$300		40

DECLINING MARKET

Amounts Invested	Share Price	Shares Acquired
$100	$10	10
100	5	20
100	4	25
$300		55

RISING MARKET

Amounts Invested	Share Price	Shares Acquired
$100	$10	10
100	20	5
100	25	4
$300		19

Average Share Cost	Average Share Cost	Average Share Cost
$300	$300	$300
40=$7.50	55=$5.45	19=$15.79

Average Share Price	Average Share Price	Average Share Price
$10+$10+$15	$10+$5+$4	$10+$20+$25
3= $8.33	3=$6.33	3=$18.33

Here's another example: If you bought a fixed number of shares each year, say 200, at various prices—$50, $25, $37.50, $62.50, and $75—until you'd invested $10,000 each year for five years, you would have spent $50,000 for 1000 shares at an average cost of $50. But if you'd dollar cost averaged, or bought $10,000 worth of stock each year at the same prices as with the fixed number of shares approach, you would have 1160 shares, each purchased for an average of $43.10. In other words, by taking the dollar cost averaging route (see Figure 6-1), you'd have 160 more shares, and your average cost per share would have been $6.90 less.

Dollar cost averaging is the exact opposite of market timing, which numerous studies have shown doesn't work. Buying and selling stocks based on guessing what the market is going to do next is as futile as lottery tickets are in retirement planning. If you could predict exactly how the market is going to act each day, you would have more riches than if you owned the goose that laid golden eggs.

The tendency is for investors to bail out of the market when it's falling and jump in when it's been trending higher for a while. But inevitably, by the time you get back in, the market has already chalked up a good gain. A University of Michigan study found that if you were out of the stock market during the best 90 days over a 31-year period, you would have missed 85 percent of the market's rise. Perhaps the biggest risk in market timing is missing out on the market's best-performing cycles. See Figure 6-2.

FIGURE 6-2. **The Risk of Being Out of the Market (Based on S&P 500's Total Returns)**

	A 1973–2002	B 1983–2002	C 1993–2002
[1] Untouched	$20,970	$10,440	$2,440
[2] Miss 10 Top-Performing Months	8,120	6,390	1,520
[3] Miss 20 Top-Performing Months	2,260	4,300	1,050

Source: Standard & Poor's Financial Communications.

In Figure 6-2, columns A, B, and C represent the growth of a $1,000 investment beginning in 1973, 1983, and 1993, and ending December 31, 2002. Row [1] shows the investment if left untouched for the entire period indicated by each column head. Row [2] shows the investment if it was pulled out during the 10 top-performing months. Row [3] shows the investment if it was pulled out during the 20 top-performing months.

Dividends for the Long Term

In addition to investing a certain amount of money each month, reinvesting dividends should be part of your dollar cost averaging program. Dividends, of course, are the cash payments that many publicly traded companies make to their shareholders out of their profits. If a company pays a dividend, you'll find its annual cash payment listed in the stock tables of major newspapers under the column heading DIV (see Chapter 7 for more on dividends).

Most people tend to fritter away their dividend checks, so it's a good idea to plow them back to buy more shares. If dividends are reinvested, they can make a dramatic difference, especially in a long-term investment program. Compounding really works here.

Case in point: If you'd invested $10,000 in the S&P 500 at the end of 1992, 10 years later your money would have grown to $20,193 (despite the horrendous 2000–2002 market). But if you'd also reinvested the dividends, your original $10,000 would have been worth $24,433. That's a 21 percent difference. See Figure 6-3.

Here's a specific example of the advantage of plowing back dividends: Consider Wilmington Trust, which provides a full range of financial services to customers in the United States and more than 50 other countries. It's been a good investment over the years. If you'd invested $10,000 in the company at year-end 1990, you would have had $23,909 at the end of 2002. However, if you'd reinvested the dividends rather than take them in cash, your stock in 2002 would have been worth $33,676, or $9767 more.

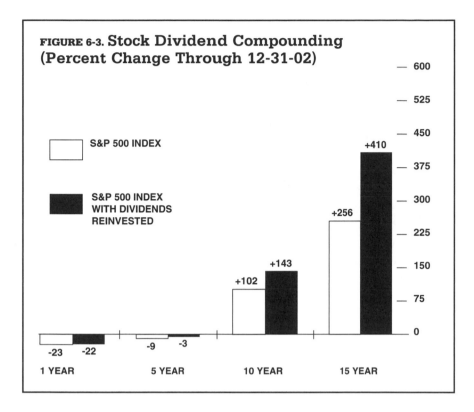

FIGURE 6-3. **Stock Dividend Compounding (Percent Change Through 12-31-02)**

- 600
- 525
- 450

☐ S&P 500 INDEX

■ S&P 500 INDEX WITH DIVIDENDS REINVESTED

- 375
- 300
- 225
- 150
- 75
- 0

+410
+256
+143
+102
-23 -22
-9 -3

1 YEAR   5 YEAR   10 YEAR   15 YEAR

Wilmington Trust, which has paid a cash dividend since 1914—and a fairly substantial one—has increased the payment for more than 20 years in a row. The current annual rate (as of July 2003) is $1.08, an increase of 52 percent since 1997. But even a stock whose dividend is small, like Mylan Labs, can bring a much higher return when the dividend is reinvested.

Mylan Labs makes generic and branded pharmaceutical products for resale by others. It has paid an annual dividend of only $0.16 since 1997. Nevertheless, over the past 10 years, your $10,000 investment would be worth $17,848 if you'd used the dividends to buy more shares. If you hadn't, you would have had $1229 less.

Hopefully you're now convinced that dividends do count. Even if a company's dividend is relatively minuscule, it pays to reinvest.

Although the payment will buy only a small fraction of a share of stock, the magic of compounding means that those fractions will add up considerably over time. The compounding comes from receiving dividends on the shares you got from reinvesting dividends.

In a nutshell, dollar cost averaging keeps you in the market, keeps you focused on your investment goals, and, best of all, gives you peace of mind.

Points to Remember

➤ The best way to make the inevitable market gyrations work for you is through dollar cost averaging. This entails investing equal amounts of money in a stock or mutual fund at regular intervals.

➤ The key to dollar cost averaging is to stick with the program through thick and thin, through roaring bull markets and gut-wrenching bear markets.

➤ The best way to dollar cost average is to have money automatically taken out of your checking or savings account each month.

➤ Dollar cost averaging is the exact opposite of market timing, which numerous studies have shown doesn't work.

➤ If you reinvest your dividends and/or capital gains distributions from mutual funds, the magic of compounding will become even more magical, and you'll reach your investment goal sooner than you think.

CHAPTER 7

The Fifth Key: Keep Your Costs Down

W hen investors brag about how much money they've made from a particular stock or mutual fund—though such boasting was noticeably absent during the 2000–2002 bear market—they've usually calculated their profit by taking the difference between what they paid for the investment and what they sold it for. Rarely mentioned is how much it cost them to purchase the stock (the commission), and, if they had a mutual fund, the additional fee they paid to the fund manager each year, or the so-called *expense ratio*, which averages a sizable 1.45 percent.

Also not usually included in the profit equation are the taxes that have to be paid on the sale of the investment. With mutual funds, that tax is not necessarily the result of a voluntary action on your part— the sale of shares in the fund. Funds each year distribute gains to you that have been realized on sales of stocks in the fund's portfolio. Whether that distribution is made in cash or is reinvested in additional shares of the fund, you pay tax on it.

If the stock or mutual fund is held less than 12 months, you wind up paying Uncle Sam anywhere from 10 percent if you're at the low end of the tax bracket to 35 percent at the high end. The average is about 25 percent. If you owned the stock or mutual fund more than 12 months, you pay a top long-term capital gains rate of 15 percent. That's only on one trade. Investors who talk up their profits are usually market in-and-outers. Their investment costs, as a result, are pretty hefty.

[71]

So, the next time you're at a cocktail party and Joe Blowhard boasts about the big stock market killing he made recently, deduct at least 20 percent from that figure.

John Bogle, the respected founder of the Vanguard Group of mutual funds, gives the following example: If the market's return is 10 percent before costs, and intermediation costs—commissions, management fees, and taxes—are about 2 percent, then investors earn 8 percent. Compounded over 50 years, 8 percent results in a $10,000 investment rising to $469,000. But at 10 percent, $10,000 becomes $1,170,000, almost three times as much. That's a huge difference. Those extra costs add up.

Direct Investment and Reinvestment Plans

One of the best ways to cut down on investment costs while building a portfolio is via direct stock purchase plans (DSPs), which permit you to buy stock directly from the companies. You don't have to go through a brokerage house, so you don't pay any commission. Most of the plans impose fees to open an account, which are typically $10. It costs a dollar to buy more shares each month; and $5 or $10, plus 10 to12 cents a share, to sell. But this is much lower than what you would pay a broker.

About 300 U.S. companies offer DSPs, and hundreds of foreign companies offer them as well. In the latter case, you buy American Depositary Receipts. The ADR, first introduced in 1927, is an investment in a non-U.S. corporation. The shares of these companies trade on a foreign exchange, while the ADRs trade on a U.S. exchange. To establish an ADR, an investment bank arranges to buy the shares on a foreign market and issue the ADRs on the U.S. markets. The bank sets the ratio of U.S. ADRs per foreign country shares. The ratio can be less than or greater than 1.0.

Joining a DSP is an easy process. You send for the prospectus, complete the authorization form that's included, and mail it to the bank or firm administering the plan. Participants receive periodic statements showing the amount of full and fractional shares purchased and the prices paid. You will receive a 1099 form at the end of the year, because even though you don't receive the dividends, they are taxable. But when you sell the shares, the dividends on which you were taxed are added to your cost basis, which reduces your capital gains tax. Thus, it's important to keep your statements, especially the year-end ones.

Form 1099 may also show some "additional income," which represents the money paid on your behalf by the company, such as fees and commissions charged by the transfer agent. These costs are considered income to you. As with reinvested dividends, it should be added to your cost of the shares, which will bring down your cost basis and thus reduce any capital gains you have to pay when you sell.

Each plan has a minimum investment, ranging from $50 to $1000. The DSPs that have high initial cash requirements usually waive the payment if you agree, when you sign up, to have $50 or $100 debited from your bank or checking account each month.

A number of DSPs and Dividend Reinvestment Plans (which we'll get to shortly) now permit you to open an Individual Retirement Account, and if you open an IRA, you don't have to worry about taxes until you start to draw down the money at a later date (you can start to withdraw without a penalty when you reach age 59½). Companies that offer IRAs include Allstate Corp., ExxonMobil, Federal National Mortgage, McDonald's, Sears, and Wal-Mart Stores.

Two useful websites for information on the various plans are www.equiserve.com and www.netstockdirect.com. These sites give details on each plan, including the telephone number to request plan materials, or you can view the prospectus online. Netstockdirect also allows you to research companies in its database of more than 1400 plans. Equiserve, the result of a merger between First Chicago Trust Company of New York and Boston Equiserve, acts as transfer agent for most of the DSPs, while on netstockdirect you can enroll in a plan online.

To build an effective DSP portfolio, stick with a mix of quality stocks. The mix should include a financial services company, a utility, an oil company, a pharmaceutical firm, and a company in each of the following sectors: technology, telecommunications, and consumer products. A list of my favorite DSPs is found in the Appendix.

DSPs are relatively new on the investment scene, having come into their own in 1994 when the SEC made it much easier and far less costly for a company to offer a DSP, and also made changes in the so-called open availability dividend reinvestment plans, or DRIPs, which have been around since the late 1960s. DRIPs differ from DSPs in that they require you to own a minimum number of shares (anywhere from one to 50) before you join. You can reinvest the dividends in both DSPs and DRIPs and make optional cash purchases.

As you can see, DSPs and DRIPs have many advantages—convenience, low cost, and automatic investing plans that give you the benefits of dollar cost averaging. But of what value are they to the issuing companies?

Obviously these plans would not be offered if they didn't aid corporations. A big benefit to companies is that DSPs and DRIPs attract small investors who are generally more loyal than big institutions such as mutual funds, banks, and pension funds. Smaller investors will hold stocks longer, which reduces volatility. At the same time, a stockholder is more likely to buy a company's products or use its services. Last but far from least, if a company issues new shares for its plan rather than buying them from the open market, it's an inexpensive way to raise capital.

Optional Cash Purchases

The optional cash purchase (OCP) feature is one of the most valuable offered by DSPs and DRIPs. In addition to reinvesting your dividends to buy more shares, OCPs enable you to build up your stock positions more quickly by purchasing shares on a regular basis. You simply write a check for at least the minimum amount, usually $50 or $100 monthly, or you can have money withdrawn from your checking or savings accounts each month. This automatic pilot approach is a far better option because it painlessly imposes discipline and you probably won't miss the money.

Some of the plans permit you to buy their stocks at a discount. These discounts range from 1 to 5 percent. Some examples: Atmos Energy offers a 3 percent discount on reinvested dividends; South Jersey Industries, 2 percent; Ball Corp., Fleming Companies, LaFarge North America, Telephone & Data Systems, and UtiliCorp United, all 5 percent; and Countrywide Credit, up to 5 percent. Since companies often change their plans, you should check with them to see if these discounts are still in effect. Of course, you wouldn't buy shares simply because you can get them on the cheap. Here's where your homework comes into play.

You can sell DSP and DRIP shares directly. Some plans may require sell instructions in writing, while others allow you to sell via the telephone, which more and more companies now permit. Check the plan prospectus for details on selling, including fees. It may take a while to receive the proceeds, however, and you don't have any control over the price at which the shares are sold. To get around these negatives, you can ask the plan agent to send you a stock certificate, and then sell the shares through a discount broker.

Some brokers will now reinvest dividends for you on a stock without a fee. They do not, however, permit you to take advantage of the valuable optional cash purchase feature of DSPs and DRIPs.

Dividends Make a Difference

In buying DSPs or DRIPs—or any stock, for that matter—I would concentrate on those that pay a dividend, preferably one that has shown consistent growth. These dividend-paying stocks let your capital grow faster.

In the roaring bull market of the late1990s, most investors were focused on capital gains and didn't care much about dividends. As a result, companies didn't feel they had to boost their payouts. Instead, corporations rewarded their stockholders via share buybacks, which reduced the number of shares outstanding, increasing per-share earnings and, in most cases, the price of the stock.

The dividend picture began to change when the market started its steep slide in 2000. In order to encourage shareholders to maintain their stock positions, companies became more generous with their dividend policies. In fact, some companies that never paid dividends before began to do so. For example, FedEx, the worldwide package delivery company, paid a dividend for the first time in 2002 amounting to $0.20 annually, while semiconductor companies Maxim Integrated Products and Microchip Technology each started to pay a small dividend of two cents a quarter. In early 2003, cash-rich Microsoft initiated an $0.08 annual dividend (boosted to $0.16 in the fall), as did medical device maker Guidant. Guidant first declared a dividend in February 2003, amounting to $0.08.

In 2002, a two-year downtrend in dividends on the S&P 500 was reversed. Dividend payments on the benchmark index rose 2.1 percent, compared with a 3.3 percent slide in 2001 and a 2.5 percent drop in 2000—the first back-to-back declines since 1970–71. From 1928 through 2002, dividends on the S&P 500 averaged a 4.7 percent increase. See Figure 7-1.

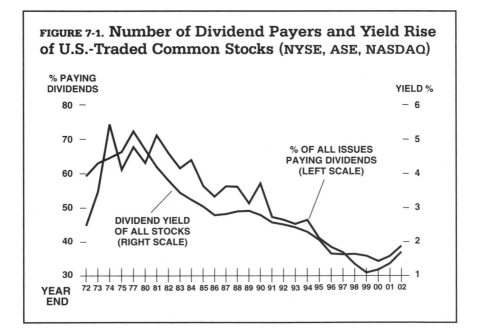

FIGURE 7-1. **Number of Dividend Payers and Yield Rise of U.S.-Traded Common Stocks (NYSE, ASE, NASDAQ)**

The most important reason why you should stick with stocks of companies that pay dividends is that they provide stability and a return on your investment when the market is in a downtrend. In 2002, for example, stocks in the S&P 500 index that paid dividends averaged a decline of 13.3 percent, compared with a 30.3 percent average plunge for the stocks in the index that didn't pay dividends. In 2001, dividend-paying stocks in the index were down only 0.1 percent, compared to a 5.4 percent decline for nondividend payers. And in 2000, the dividend payers rose 15.7 percent, compared with a 2.2 percent drop for S&P 500 stocks that didn't pay dividends. On average, over the three bear-market years 2000 through 2002, the dividend payers in the index roughly broke even, while the nondividend stocks were down close to 35 percent.

Another reason to go with dividend-paying stocks: Once paid, the dividends are yours to keep. In other words, "a bird in the hand is worth two in the bush." Capital gains, on the other hand, remain potential until your shares are sold. Also, aside from options strategies, which risk the sale of some or all of your holdings, dividends are the only way to profit from your stocks without reducing or eliminating your ownership stake in the company.

Further, dividends represent a tangible return to shareholders and can't be manipulated, as is the case with earnings. We've seen World-Com, Enron, and Xerox forced to restate profits because of questionable accounting practices. Others include PNC Financial, the Pittsburgh-based bank holding company, which was required by the SEC to restate earnings because the company erroneously recognized $55 million of gain on the sale of a business unit; and ConAgra, one of the largest U.S. food processors, which was forced to reduce profits by $123 million after fictitious sales and misreporting earnings for the company's United AgriProducts subsidiary. According to the U.S. General Accounting Office, about 10 percent of all publicly traded companies have restated their earnings at least once since 1997.

Dividends are either paid or they are not paid, increased or not increased; there can be no hanky-panky.

A strong dividend history also can point the way to profitable investments. Companies with long histories of annual dividend increases usually enjoy solid earnings growth, since they wouldn't be able to regularly boost dividends without steady profits. See Figure 7-2. Most of these companies are accorded a Standard & Poor's quality ranking of at least A-, which indicates above-average growth and stability of earnings over at least the past 10 years. (For a list of companies that offer DSPs or DRIPs that have been longtime dividend payers and have steadily hiked their payments, see the Appendix.)

Of course, companies can stop paying dividends or reduce them at any time. For example, Xerox, which paid dividends since 1930, suspended them in 2001, and Corning also eliminated its dividend in 2001, after paying one since 1881. In early 2003, Goodyear, the number one U.S. maker of tires, which has been around for a century, stopped paying dividends for the first time since the Great Depression. But corporations that regularly increase their dividends try very hard to maintain their records. You can imagine why: If a company that has hiked payments every year for a decade or more suddenly holds its dividend steady, it's a sign that the nature of the business may be changing or that something is amiss.

Dividends have become even more attractive with passage of the Jobs and Growth Tax Relief Reconcilation Act of 2003, signed into law by President George W. Bush in late May 2003. President Bush had wanted to completely eliminate the dividend tax, since corporations pay taxes on profits, out of which they pay dividends, and then individuals pay taxes on the dividends when they receive them. While the new tax law does not change the taxes that corporations pay on earnings, it does reduce a shareholder's dividend tax rate to 15 percent through 2008 for shareholders in the top four federal ordinary income tax brackets, and to 5 percent through 2007 (0 percent in 2008) for shareholders in the 10 percent and 15 percent ordinary income tax brackets.

These rates, considerably lower than the ordinary income tax rates that were applied to dividends before the Growth Tax Relief Reconcilation Act of 2003, have materially increased demand for dividend-paying stocks. Many observers believe that the 15 percent rate on dividends will be extended beyond 2008, since few politicians would want suffer the consequences of turning back the clock.

FIGURE 7-2. High-Quality Long-Term Dividend Payers

	Ticker Symbol	Quality Ranking	*S&P Index	Dividend Paid Since	Percent Dividend Increase 1992–2002
AmSouth Bancorp	ASO	A-	500	1943	197
Anheuser-Busch	BUD	A+	500	1932	160
Avon Products	AVP	A	500	1919	111
BB&T Corp.	BBT	A-	500	1934	364
Bank of New York	BK	A-	500	1934	300
Bemis Co.	BMS	A+	500	1922	126
Chubb Corp.	CB	B+	500	1902	77
Coca-Cola	KO	A-	500	1893	186
Compass Bancshares	CBSS	A+	Mid	1939	245
Ecolab Inc.	ECL	A	500	1936	241
ExxonMobil	XOM	A-	500	1882	30
Gannett Co.	GCI	A	500	1929	52
Gillette Co.	G	A-	500	1906	282
Hershey Foods	HSY	A-	500	1930	153
Johnson & Johnson	JNJ	A+	500	1944	273
Johnson Controls	JCI	A+	500	1887	125
Marsh & McLennan	MMC	A	500	1923	155
McCormick & Co	MKC	A-	Mid	1929	132
Mercantile Bankshares	MRBK	A	Mid	1909	208
National City Corp	NCC	A	500	1936	160
PPG Industries	PPG	A-	500	1899	83
PepsiCo	PEP	A	500	1952	140
Pfizer Inc	PFE	A+	500	1901	333
Pitney Bowes	PBI	A	500	1934	203
Procter & Gamble	PG	A	500	1891	204
Progress Energy	PGN	A-	500	1937	42
Questar Corp.	STR	A-	Mid	1935	42
SouthTrust Corp.	SOTR	A+	500	1944	300
Walgreen Co.	WAG	A+	500	1933	114
Wilmington Trust	WL	A+	Mid	1914	132

*500-In S&P 500 Index; Mid-In S&P MidCap 400 Index.

Also as part of the new tax law, long-term capital gains rates were reduced. Gains on the sale of securities held for more than one year (the definition of long-term capital gains) for shareholders in the top four federal tax brackets dropped to 15 percent from 20 percent through 2008. Shareholders in the 10 percent and 15 percent bracket, formerly taxed at a 10 percent rate, are taxed at 5 percent through 2007 (0 percent in 2008). Short-term capital gains continue to be taxed at the higher ordinary income rates.

In spite of the lower tax rates on dividends, some investors still don't like them. They believe that a company should be plowing back profits to make it grow, rather than paying out dividends.

Warren Buffett's Berkshire Hathaway has never paid a dividend, though the company has purchased a number of stocks that do have a payout. A *Wall Street Journal* story in 2002 entitled "I Hate Dividends," written by a former hedge-fund manager, maintained that companies that pay dividends are admitting that they have nothing better to do with their money. A response to this is that many non-dividend-paying companies have had dismal records in investing their profits. In most cases, they would have been better off paying dividends than using the money to make acquisitions, which often prove to be nightmares.

There are many examples of acquisitions gone awry. One of those is the AOL–Time Warner marriage, which has turned out to be one of the all-time worst mergers. From early January 2000, when the combination was announced, to early 2003, the company's value, in terms of its stock, plummeted $160 billion, and it took a $54 billion write-down in the first three months of 2002—the biggest quarterly loss ever. In the fourth quarter of 2002, AOL wrote off $46 billion, for a grand total of $100 billion for the year.

Another company, Nortel Networks, a leading suppler of telecommunications equipment, went on an acquisition binge starting in 1997 (most of the acquisitions were paid with Nortel's inflated stock), and Nortel wound up writing off more than $12 billion. Still another dud was the purchase of NCR by AT&T; Ma Bell finally spun off NCR to shareholders.

My opinion: For a long-term investor, sticking with stocks that pay dividends and boost them regularly is a sure road to financial success.

Cutting Mutual Fund Fees

Now that we've looked at how to keep your costs down by getting into DSPs and DRIPs (preferably those that pay dividends), let's explore how to save money on mutual funds.

First lesson: Think twice before buying a mutual fund from a broker. You'll inevitably pay a "load," or sales commission, anywhere from 3 or 4 percent to more than 8 percent.

Consider a $10,000 investment in a fund with a front-end load (the sales charge when you buy the fund) of 8.5 percent. It results in an $850 sales charge, with only $9150 going into the fund. The load actually represents 9.3 percent of the net funds invested. Further, the effect of the load, if paid up front, is not diminished as quickly as many believe, even if a load fund is held for many years. If the money paid for the load had been working for you from the very beginning, as in a no-load fund (which doesn't have a sales charge), it would have been compounding over the entire period.

The various classes of mutual funds, designated by letters, reflect their different fee structure. See Figure 7-3. Generally, class A has a front-end load, class B has a back-end load, or redemption fee, and class C (called level load) has no front or back loads but higher annual charges over time than class B. As we've stressed, buy only those funds that are no-load and that have a low expense ratio.

Also, funds have several different sneaky ways of tacking on sales charges, such as back-end loads, deferred sales charges, or redemption fees, all of which mean you pay when you sell the fund. And we have the so-called 12b-1 fee, named for the section of the Investment Company Act that permits it. That little extra allows the fund's investment adviser to use fund assets to pay for distribution costs, including advertising, mailing of fund literature, and sales commissions paid to brokers.

FIGURE 7-3. Characteristics of Mutual Fund Share Classes

Share Class	Sales Charge	12b-1 Fee	Investment Advice Provided	Appropriate for
Class A	Sales charge is up-front fee, typically 2.5–5.5% of NAV at time of purchase	Usually not charged	Yes	Long-term investment
Class B	Contingent-deferred sales charge collected when shares redeemed, typically 5% of NAV declining to 0% after 6–8 years; sales charge may be assessed on NAV existing at time of purchase or at time of redemption, depending on the fund	Typically 0.75% annually of NAV	Yes	Investment held 4–6 years; longer if shares convert to Class A after that time
Class C	Typically a sales charge of 1–2% of NAV each year	0–0.75% of NAV annually	Yes	Short-term investment of 5 years or less
No-Load	None	May not charge more than 0.25% annually	No	Investor who does not necessarily need assistance of broker or financial advisor in selecting investments

Those are the explicit costs. There is also the implicit cost of trading. Most funds have a high turnover (buying and selling many stocks), which means high commission costs. These trading costs can amount to 2 percent or more of the fund's assets annually. According to Morningstar, funds with extremely high turnovers—400 percent or more—can generate costs of 8 percent and higher.

Also, as mentioned earlier, there's another cost: Unless you have your mutual fund in a tax-deferred account, such as an IRA, you must pay taxes on the capital gains and dividends that are distributed each year. Even if you bought the fund just before a distribution is made, you still have to pay taxes.

Last but not least, there's the fee you have to pay to a fund manager for managing the fund, even though management is often poorly executed. This fee represents the largest portion of a fund's operating expenses. All of a fund's fees—adviser's fees, legal and accounting fees, 12b-1 fees—are called the *expense ratio*. You can calculate a fund's expense ratio by dividing its annual expenses by its average net assets, though it's easier if you refer to the prospectus, which is required to list it.

The expense ratio can make a big difference in how much profit you wind up with. For example, $10,000 invested in a fund earning 5 percent with an expense ratio of 1.68 percent would be worth $13,863 in 10 years. If the expense ratio were only 0.56 percent, you would have $15,441, or $1578 more. Be wary of a mutual fund that has an expense ratio higher than 1 percent, and, to repeat, think twice about buying a fund that imposes a sales charge. Check the prospectus carefully for all charges. Published investment returns for funds usually deduct annual fees from the performance numbers, but not front-end or deferred sales charges.

There are several free websites that provide online calculators so you can compare mutual fund costs. The SEC website, www.sec.gov, provides a combined load and cost calculator; www.quicken.com permits you to calculate and compare fund costs in its Investing Basics quick-answer section; and www.smartmoney.com offers a basic fund-fee and load analyzer in its Tools section.

By far the best funds, in my opinion, are those that are tied to an index, such as the Vanguard and T. Rowe Price 500 funds (which mimic the S&P 500 index), or, even better, their Total Stock Market Index funds (which are based on the Wilshire 5000 index). According to Standard & Poor's Fund Advisor, more than 63 percent of all large-cap equity funds were unable to beat the S&P 500 index benchmark over the 1998–2002 period. Over the longer term, the performance of managed funds is just as bleak.

These no-load index funds give you diversification at a low cost. The expense ratios are well below 1 percent. Another plus: The funds are tax efficient since there's relatively little turnover. The funds trade only when a stock is added to or deleted from the indexes. (For more details on these funds, see Figures 7-4, 7-5, and the Appendix.)

FIGURE 7-4. **Equity Funds That Beat the S&P 500 Index**

Year	S&P 500 Return	% That Beat Index
1987	5.18	26%
1988	16.61	46%
1989	31.69	21%
1990	–3.10	38%
1991	30.47	57%
1992	7.62	58%
1993	10.08	61%
1994	1.32	24%
1995	37.53	15%
1996	22.95	23%
1997	33.35	10%
1998	28.58	17%
1999†	21.04	49%
2000	–9.10	65%
2001	–11.88	48%

*Domestic universe excludes balanced (or hybrid) and sector funds; it includes index funds and multiple share classes.
†Data from 1999 includes survivorship bias.

Exchange-Traded Funds

Exchange-traded funds (ETFs), which are relatively new to the investment scene, are also attractive. These are a basket of stocks that trade on an exchange like a single stock and are usually based on a market index. For example, "Spiders," more formally known as Standard & Poor's Depositary Receipts (SPDRs), tracks the performance of the S&P 500 index.

FIGURE 7-5. **A Choice of Market Indexes**

S&P 500

500 large-cap stocks that make up the components of the U.S. economy

Russell 2000

The stocks of 2,000 U.S. small-capitalization companies

EAFE

Stock markets in Europe, the Far East, and Australasia

FT 100

100 stocks traded in London

Nikkei 225

A mix of stocks traded on the Tokyo Stock Exchange

Wilshire 5000

A broad-based index of 5000 U.S. companies

Spiders, the first ETF, began trading on the American Stock Exchange in January 1993. Today, there are more than 35 ETFs that track market indexes, with combined assets of over $50 billion, plus ETFs of stocks in different sectors. Portfolios called "Diamonds," holding all 30 stocks of the Dow Jones Industrials, appeared in January 1998, and in that same year came a high-flying replica of the tech-heavy Nasdaq 100 called "Cubes" (ticker symbol QQQ).

ETF investors avoid the redemption fees and other restrictions applied by index mutual funds to discourage frequent trading, but do pay brokerage commission on both the purchase and sale of funds traded as stocks. Unlike closed-end funds (which also trade like stocks), that trade at a premium or discount to their net asset value—the NAV, which is total assets minus total liabilities—ETFs are priced in line with their intrinsic value because institutions constantly look for arbitrage opportunities.

For example, if the price of the underlying stocks goes above the price of the ETF, institutional investors will trade a lower-priced "creation unit," or basket of securities, to the ETF in exchange for the higher-priced securities. Small investors, as a result, can get in or out of the shares anytime at a price close to the NAV. This is helpful when the market is taking a dive. Mutual fund holders can only get out of their investment at the closing price on any day. Also, ETFs can be sold short (which I don't recommend), even on a downtick.

Another ETF advantage is that they're tax efficient. This is because the fund can unload the lowest-cost shares on an institution that wants to trade them for so-called creation units; the capital gain goes to the institution and not to ETF shareholders. With mutual funds, sales of stock can be triggered when the fund needs to raise cash to meet redemptions. Any capital gains from those trades are passed directly to shareholders.

A disadvantage of ETFs is that you have to pay a commission to buy them, and, unlike mutual funds, ETFs don't necessarily trade at the net asset values of their underlying holdings; that is, an ETF could potentially trade above or below the value of the underlying portfolios. Also, as with stocks, there is a bid-ask spread; for instance, you

FIGURE 7-6 ETFs vs. Index Funds

Characteristics	ETFs	Index Mutual Funds
Is trading continuous?	Yes	No
Can be sold short?	Yes	No
Leverage	Can borrow 50%	None
Expense ratio	Extremely low	Very low
Trading costs	Stock commission	None
Dividend reinvestment	No	Yes
Automatic investment program	No	Yes
Tax efficiency	Extremely good	Very good

might buy the ETF for $25.25 but only be able to sell it for $25.00. Figure 7-6 campares ETF and index funds.

Investing directly with a mutual fund is generally more advantageous, particularly in tax-deferred accounts, or if you want to invest automatically every month, which I recommend.

Websites that offer detailed information on ETFs include www.amex.com, www.ishares.com, www.holdrs.com, and also www. streettracks.com.

Points to Remember

> ➤ Keeping investment costs as low as possible is an essential part of meeting your long-term financial goals.

> ➤ Direct Investment Plans (DSPs) and Dividend Reinvestment Plans (DRIPs) are excellent ways to invest inexpensively. Their automatic withdrawal plans from your bank or checking account for optional cash purchases (OCPs) make you a disciplined investor, and you get the benefits of dollar cost averaging.

> ➤ Concentrate on DSPs and DRIPs that pay dividends. Dividend-paying stocks let your capital grow faster and provide stability and a return on your investment when the market is in a down-trend. Dividends represent a tangible return on your money and can't be manipulated, as is the case with earnings.

> ➤ Buying mutual funds through a broker entails commissions. Buying no-load doesn't.

> ➤ Before buying a no-load fund, make sure its expense ratio is well below 1 percent.

> ➤ Index funds are usually your best bet.

> ➤ Exchange-traded funds (ETFs) are somewhat similar to index funds, although you can't set up an automatic debit plan.

> ➤ Keep good records; it's essential that you hang on to year-end statements.

CHAPTER 8

The Sixth Key: Know When to Sell

D eciding when to sell a stock or mutual fund is probably the toughest aspect of investing. The tendency is for investors to stay married to a stock or fund. But even the bluest of the blue chips can wind up in the dog house.

The classic example is AT&T, at one time the refuge of widows and orphans, a company that was able to pay dividends throughout the Great Depression of the 1930s. By 1983, when AT&T had become a top choice for retirement portfolios, the U.S. government forced the company's breakup. At the year's close, Ma Bell had gathered its 22 local phone services into seven holding companies and sent them off on their own. The new AT&T was a long distance provider that could compete in unregulated markets, and it became more of a growth company. It got into other businesses, including computers, cellular phones, the Universal credit card, and broadband—a high-speed Internet connection that provides access to the Web up to 50 times faster than a dial-up connection.

AT&T turned into a mixed bag with mixed results. The stock was no longer a safe, reliable dividend payer. In fact, the annual dividend was slashed to $0.15 in 2002 from $0.88. And after reaching a high of $66 in 1999, the shares plummeted to $12 in 2002, an 82 percent decline. Although the lower price partly reflected several chunks of the company that were spun off to shareholders, it also was the result of weakness in the long-distance market, a high debt load, and scrutiny over AT&T's accounting practices.

Finally, in a move to boost the price, a one-for-five reverse stock split was declared in November 2002; that is, every five shares a shareholder owned became one share. Reverse splits are usually made only by highly questionable penny stocks.

Monitor Your Investments

The point is, never buy a stock and then forget about it. Warren Buffett was once asked when to sell a stock, and he replied, "Never." That's probably the only part of his investment philosophy I don't agree with. Just as with a marriage, it's no disgrace to divorce an investment that isn't working out.

Unfortunately, the vast majority of investors either sell too early or too late. Although there are no sure-fire formulas to tell you when the time is right to sell a stock or a fund, several guidelines can be useful to weed out your portfolio.

Most important, you should periodically take an objective look at your investments. Ask yourself if the reasons you initially bought a particular stock still apply today. If you purchased shares of a utility for income, is the company continuing to increase its dividend? Or has the utility gotten into a riskier business? If so, the dividend may be in jeopardy as the company plows back all or most of its earnings into the business.

If you've owned a stock for many years, ask yourself from time to time: Would I buy this stock today? Are the company's fundamentals as favorable as when I purchased the stock originally?

Earnings and Dividend Growth Rates

If a company's earnings or dividend growth rate starts to decline after three or four years of increase, that should be a red flag. Stocks are mainly valued on the discounted value of a company's future earnings. So, in order for a stock to show a steady climb, the company has to regularly improve its profits. Top-line (sales) growth, as well as cash flow, should also be in steady uptrends. If not, think about dumping the shares.

Monitor a stock's price-earnings ratio. A P/E higher than its three-year average should raise another red flag. Find out if the higher P/E is justified. If the company's sales, earnings, and market share are growing, then the richer P/E is warranted. If not, perhaps the general level of inflation and interest rates have fallen, which can account for an increase in P/Es across the board. But if these have not occurred, put in a sell order.

You should also study a company's balance sheet for clues to its health. The balance sheet is a key financial statement that is reported to investors at least once a year. It provides information on what the company owns (assets), what it owes (liabilities), and the value of the business to its stockholders—or the shareholders' equity (total assets minus total liabilities).

Pay close attention to a company's debt levels. The debt-to-capitalization ratio will tell you if the firm is becoming too leveraged—that is, too debt ridden. To find the ratio, take the total market value of the company—number of shares outstanding times the stock price—including any long-term debt, and then figure out what portion of this value is made up of long-term debt. If the percentage of long-term debt to total capitalization (or enterprise value) is steadily climbing or is high relative to other companies in the same field, that's another red flag.

Management Changes and Noncore Acquistions

In addition to a company's financial situation, pay attention to any management changes. If several top executives leave a company after a long, successful stint, that could signal trouble. For example, when the well-respected CEO, Jack Welch, retired from General Electric, the stock went into a tailspin.

Another selling clue is if the company has grown mainly through noncore acquisitions rather than through internal growth. Studies indicate that two-thirds of acquisitions don't work out. The word "synergy" often crops up when a merger is announced. But it's not too often that a combination of two different companies results in "the whole being greater than the sum of its parts."

Market Share and Stock Price

Also, if a company's market share begins to erode for a variety of reasons, such as newer, stronger entrants in a particular field or, in the case of drug companies, a valuable pharmaceutical going off patent, it may be time to abandon ship.

Monitor the stock price. If a stock falls, say, 25 percent from your purchase price, you should seriously consider getting rid of it. It's not uncommon for investors to continue to hang onto a stock as it drops, even when it plummets 50 percent or more. Lucent Technologies is an example. Because of its fine reputation and association with AT&T—it was considered the best part of that company after various divisions were spun off—relatively few people, especially long-term holders, bailed out as the shares plunged from their high of $84 in 1999 to below a dollar in 2002. In October of that year, because of the low price—which meant that the shares could be delisted from the New York Stock Exchange—Lucent, like AT&T, announced that its board of directors would seek shareholder approval for a reverse stock split.

Stop-Loss Orders

You could issue a stop-loss order with your broker to limit any losses. For example, you can set one up for 10 percent below the price you paid for the stock. Then, if you were to buy General Electric at $40, you enter a stop-loss order for $35 immediately after purchasing the shares. That means if GE falls below $35, your shares would be sold at the prevailing market price.

The downside of a stop-loss order is that the stop price could be set in motion by a short-term fluctuation in the price of a stock. For this reason, it's essential that you pick a stop-loss percentage that permits a stock to fluctuate from day to day, while preventing as much downside risk as possible. Also, once your stop price is reached, your stop-loss order becomes a market order—an order to sell at the best available current price—and the price at which you sell may be much different from the stop-loss price. This is particularly the case in a fast-moving market, where stock prices can change quickly, as in the 1990s bull market.

An important point to remember: A sharp drop in a stock often means that some investors are dumping shares because they know something you don't.

Avoid Get-Even-itis

Don't hang on to a stock after a big decline, hoping it will come back. If one of your holdings plunges 50 percent, you may think you can hang on to recoup your loss, but the stock has to rise 100 percent in order for you to break even.

Sun Microsystems, for instance, was a hot tech stock in 2000, when it reached a high of $64. Three years later its price languished at about three dollars per share. Sun's stock would have had to climb more than 2000 percent to get back to the level of its glory days.

The morale is: Set a limit on how much of a loss you can take, say, 20 to 25 percent. In a nutshell, avoid "get-even-itis."

When you take a loss, regard it as a good tax move. You can take any loss and apply it dollar for dollar against any gains you have. If you're not taking any gains, you can apply up to $3000 of any loss against ordinary income. If you still have losses left over, you can carry them forward indefinitely. In effect, think of the process as making lemonade out of your lemons.

Other Reasons to Sell

When a stock position becomes too large relative to your entire portfolio, it can be time to sell. A rule of thumb is that a single stock should not represent more than 10 percent of your portfolio. That doesn't mean you have to dump all the shares of a big winner; sell enough to make the stock a lower percentage of your portfolio.

Another reason to sell is if a better opportunity presents itself and you need the money to buy the shares. Make sure, though, that the potential in the new stock is there. You don't want to get rid of a good performer to take a gamble on an iffy situation.

Peter Lynch has nicely summed up reasons to sell:

"You should ask yourself what inning it is in a company's life. If it's a growth company, the game might last 10 to 30 more years. But eventually, growth companies have to come up with a new story. Cyclicals, such as paper companies or steel makers, are different. When a cyclical stock goes from good to terrific, what's left? It's not going to stay terrific for long. If you're in that industry, your edge is that you can see it slowing down. You see that inventories are building up or that competition is stealing market share. When the balance sheet starts to slip, I'm out."

To Sell or Not to Sell

Deciding when to sell is no easy process, but after you've been in the market awhile, you should develop good instincts. Always pay attention to those instincts. On the flip side, here are reasons *not* to sell:

➤ The price hasn't budged in months. Don't concentrate on short-term price movements; the company's fundamentals are key.

➤ Bad news that could prove to be merely temporary. Delve into the nature of the adverse news. Will it affect the company's business or standing over the long term? If not, stick with it.

➤ You have a big loss in a bad market. Before you sell, make sure it's the company, not the market, that has a problem.

➤ You have a huge gain. Don't pull the trigger too fast—the company's fundamentals may warrant the higher price. Earnings may be accelerating, or a new product may show much promise. If the fundamentals are sound and you still have the urge to sell, compromise and sell only half your position. Many investors make the mistake of selling stocks that are rising, without taking into account the company's continued growth prospects, and they keep the stocks that are falling, hoping they'll come back. Most of the time, it should be the other way around.

If you're a buy and hold investor—which I hope you are, or aspire to be—that doesn't mean you should forget about your investments. As was stressed above, give your portfolio a regular checkup, which should take place at least annually. And that may involve making a sell decision. Using the guidelines in this chapter will help make the decision process easier.

Points to Remember

➤ Although when to sell is probably the hardest investment decision to make, there are certain guidelines you can follow that will make it easier.

➤ Don't feel you have to be married to a stock or mutual fund. Take an objective look at your investments periodically.

➤ Ask yourself if the reasons you bought the stock originally still apply today.

➤ Look for red flags. These include an earnings or dividend growth rate that starts to decline after three or four years, a P/E ratio higher than its three-year average, management changes, a weakening balance sheet, and a sharply falling stock price.

➤ Regard a stock sale at a loss as a tax maneuver. You can take the loss and apply it dollar for dollar against any gains you have, then you can apply up to $3000 of any remaining loss against your ordinary income that year.

➤ If a stock position amounts to more than 10 percent of your portfolio, sell some of the shares.

➤ Consider issuing a stop-loss order 10 to 15 percent below the current level, depending on the volatility of the stock.

➤ There are reasons *not* to sell a stock: (1) The price hasn't budged in months. Don't concentrate on short-term price movements; the company's fundamentals are key. (2) Bad news that could prove to be merely temporary. Delve into the nature of the adverse news. (3) You have a big loss in a bad market. Before you sell, make sure it's the company, not the market, that has a problem. (4) You have a huge gain. Don't pull the trigger too fast; the company's fundamentals may warrant the higher price.

➤ Give your portfolio a regular checkup, which should take place at least annually and may involve making a sell decision.

CHAPTER 9

Making Investment Decisions

I n my forty plus years of studying and investing in the security markets, one of the most important lessons I've learned is not to be swayed by others in making investment decisions. Do your own thing, and do it as simply as possible. Turn a jaundiced eye to market "experts," and don't follow brokers' advice blindly—many are mainly interested in extracting as much in commission fees as they can, and often push their firms' product of the day.

As for analysts, some of them take the easy way out. They're too lazy or too overworked to dig into a company and do an in-depth dissection. Instead they take management's pronouncements as gospel truth, spewing back the CEO's or CFO's predictions of sales and earnings or lifting material from the company's annual and quarterly reports and press releases without bothering to check with the company's customers and suppliers. As Chuck Hill, director of research at Thomson First Call, says: "Analysts who only report what they've learned from company executives are basically stenographers." So, be aware of how well a particular analyst's recommendations have performed in the past.

That brings us to those analysts who serve two masters—investment bankers and brokerage customers—and usually wind up catering to the fat-fee investment side of the business. At the turn of the millennium, there was no shortfall of such analysts, who have since then come under fire for highly questionable work habits.

A Plague of Analysts

Jack Grubman, former star telecom analyst at Citigroup's Salomon Smith Barney who earned as much as $20 million a year, epitomized the lack of integrity that characterized the late 1990s. Grubman rated WorldCom, which used Salomon as an investment banker, as a buy until the stock lost 90 percent of its value, at which point he downgraded it to "neutral." The phone and data-services company, with which Grubman had a close relationship—including sitting in on board of directors' meetings—was accused of a "smorgasbord" of fraudulent accounting adjustments.

Similarly, Grubman championed Global Crossing until it slithered into bankruptcy court. His tardy "neutral" rating or other euphemisms for "sell" came much too late to help most of the investors who relied on his analytical abilities. When Grubman resigned in August 2002, his severance package was estimated at $32 million. At the end of 2002 he had to at least give some of that up when he was fined $15 million (which amounted to a slap on the wrist) and in addition was barred for life from serving as a securities analyst.

The 800-pound gorilla in the brokerage business—Merrill Lynch—had its share of unethical analysts too, as evidenced by a number of infamous e-mails that were recovered by New York Attorney General Eliot Spitzer. Some examples: Henry Blodgett, another star analyst at the time, wrote in an e-mail that Excite@Home "is such a piece of crap," while at the same time recommending accumulation of the stock. Blodgett was also recommending Lifeminders, about which he wrote: "I can't believe what a POS (piece of s—) that thing is." Other e-mails he wrote were equally as odious.

At a press conference, Merrill Lynch's chairman and CEO said the company was embarrassed by the e-mails and apologized for them. In a settlement between the New York attorney general and Merrill Lynch, Merrill also paid $100 million in fines and agreed to change the way its analysts do business.

Conflicts of Interest on Wall Street

Federal and state regulators also fined other large investment firms to settle allegations of conflict of interest and unfair business practices. Ten of the biggest, including Morgan Stanley, Lehman Brothers, J.P. Morgan, Bear Stearns, and Goldman Sachs, were socked with more than $1.4 billion in penalties. The heaviest fine—$350 million—was paid by Citigroup's Salomon Smith Barney.

To address the conflict of interest problem, the landmark settlement also required the largest securities firms to pay $450 million over five years to buy research reports from independent research companies that are not involved in the investment banking business. Those securities firms must contract with no fewer than three independent research companies. As a result, investors will have access to at least one independent research report in addition to the stock research published by their investment companies, and they will also be able to access that research online. In addition, the settlement provides funds for investor education, and brokerage firms are required to put stock ratings from different sources on statements investors are sent after they buy a stock.

Finally, the agreement severs the links between researchers and investment banks. Citigroup, for instance, complied before the official settlement by splitting off Salomon Smith Barney from its investment banking business.

Buyer Beware

However, separating research from investment banking will not totally solve the problem. Analysts will still publish research reports that brokers will give to customers, and it's likely that some brokers will push stocks that analysts recommend, even if the stocks are dogs. Keep in mind that stock brokerage companies are like any other marketer pitching products, so do your own investigative work. Don't rely solely on Wall Street research. Just as you wouldn't rush to the phone to buy a Whiz-Bang combination potato peeler/screwdriver advertised in a TV infomercial, you should also be skeptical of some of the research. Some cynics say that analysts are for entertainment purposes only.

New York Attorney General Spitzer conducted a study showing that from 1999 to 2002 most of the analysts who were deemed the best by institutional investors actually turned in lackluster performances when judged solely on their stock picks. In both 2001 and 2002, only one of the 51 analysts ranked the highest by *Institutional Investor* would have also been ranked the best stock picker in his or her industry. The magazine's poll considered how analysts dealt with institutional clients, as well as their stock picking ability. That Jack Grubman was chosen by institutional investors as their favorite telecommunications analyst was one of the reasons for his rise to renown and the big bucks.

With criminal and civil actions against offenders, plus new laws and greater oversight, the situation should improve considerably over time.

As for the TV talking heads, I wouldn't pay too much attention to them. The tube commentators may look terrific and appear knowledgeable, but many of them know little more than you do. The financial channels need to fill a lot of air time, and much of that air time is fluff. Then, too, there are guests who may have an interest in stocks they're touting (even though interviewers now usually ask the interviewee if his or her company has a position in the stocks under discussion).

If you do hear of an investment on television that appeals to you, regard it only as a starting point. Again, do your homework, and lots of it. What legendary investor Bernard Baruch said many years ago still rings true: "My success emphasized one thing—the importance of getting the facts free from tips, inside dope, and wishful thinking. Before you buy a security, find out everything you can about the company, its management, competitors, earnings, and possibilities for growth." Get hard facts before you buy or sell stocks.

Research Is As Research Does

Rather than watching the self-described TV sages, it's more worthwhile to read publications such as the *Wall Street Journal, Barron's, Investor's Business Daily,* and *Business Week* on a regular basis.

These periodicals are jargon free and are written so clearly that even an investment neophyte can understand them. But even with these reputable publications, the research and data should be regarded as a starting point, a foundation on which to base your own research.

You might move on from these publications to sources of independent research such as Morningstar, Value Line, and Standard & Poor's. And if you ignore the buy, hold, and sell advice of the brokers, much of their research is also worthwhile.

Here are a few suggestions and cautionary tips concerning research:

➤ Regardless of the source, read all reports with a questioning if not a skeptical mind. Pay close attention to negatives that may be buried in the copy.

➤ Always draw your own conclusions.

➤ Don't make an investment decision based on just one report. Be thorough in your research.

➤ Don't let emotions get in your way. Your research should be fact-based and your judgment rational. To this end, write down in a clear, concise manner exactly why you've decided to buy a particular stock.

➤ Periodically, consult your own rationale for buying the stock to see if your reasons still stand up.

Favor the Long-Term Approach

In all my years of investing, I've found that the best way to not "sweat the small stuff" is to take the long view. Just holding on to solid stocks and low-cost, low-turnover mutual funds will make you more money over the long term than almost any other method. If you set reasonable investment objectives, go with quality stocks and index-type funds, and you're content to grow rich slowly, success is all but assured. To put it another way, I advocate buy, hold, and monitor.

Not only should your perspective be a long one, it should also be optimistic. As we've pointed out, historically, the market's basic trend is upward. Every bear market has been followed by a bull market, and the gains have always outweighed the losses. The market has usually reached a bottom when earnings, stock prices, and psychology look their gloomiest. And, of course, the opposite is true. The market normally is at its peak when the economy is on a tear, earnings are going through the roof, and investors are euphoric.

To protect yourself in bear markets, diversification is key. Don't panic nor get caught up in the market's latest fad, such as the Internet stocks that were red hot in the late 1990s and became stone cold dead in the market in the early 2000s. If you keep your portfolio balanced with growth and value stocks, money market and fixed-income securities, you'll survive a down market in pretty good shape. For example, in the 1973–74 bear market—a 48 percent plunge over a 21-month period—an investor whose $100,000 portfolio consisted of 60 percent stocks and 40 percent bonds lost $29,000, compared to a $48,000 loss for an investor with a $100,000 portfolio that was 100 percent in stocks.

Rebalancing your portfolio, which we went into in an earlier chapter, is another way to protect yourself. A study by T. Rowe Price shows the benefits of this strategy. If an investor had put $100,000 in the market in 1994, splitting it 60 percent stocks, 30 percent bonds, and 10 percent cash, and never rebalanced, at the market's peak on March 27, 2000, the investment would have been worth more than $271,000. By July 2002 the investment would have fallen to $204,000. On the other hand, if the investor had rebalanced anytime the portfolio got more than 5 percentage points above or below the target allocation, the money would have grown to $255,000 by the peak, and dropped to only $215,000 in the bear market.

With the Herd or Against the Crowd?

Going against the crowd is another strategy that often pays, though it can also be riskier and judgment is key.

There have been many instances of anticrowd investing that proved lucrative. One of the more dramatic was health care stocks in 1993, when investors bailed out of the group because of concern that the Clinton health-care plan would savage the profits of pharmaceutical and medical companies. The plan never got off the ground, and the stocks outperformed the S&P 500 by a wide margin for the next seven years.

Another instance: investors who stuck with tobacco stocks in the mid-1980s, when product liability suits were threatened, did well. Of course, when the suits began to materialize, that was the time to get out.

And, to repeat, in the late 1990s, investors who went against the crowd when the high-tech/Internet craze was in full force were the big winners.

Don't Delay

The key element in investing, and the point I began hammering at in the first chapter, and will continue to hammer at until the last, is that you have to set up an automatic investment plan as soon as possible—like yesterday. As the New York State lottery commercial says, "You've got to be in it to win it" (though you should never be in any lottery, as we've discussed). And the best way—the no-brainer approach—is to have money withdrawn from your checking or savings account regularly and put into sound mutual funds and high-quality stocks with favorable fundamentals. This will provide built-in discipline, and you'll probably never miss the dollars that are siphoned off each month into your "get rich slowly" accounts.

The stock market, about which there is nothing mysterious, offers the best way to build wealth. Stick with your investment plan—the simpler, the better—and don't be frightened off by poor markets. Index funds and high-quality, dividend-paying stocks won't make you a killing, but over the long run they'll help you meet your financial goals with a minimum amount of aggravation.

Points to Remember

➤ Make your own investment decisions, based on sound, solid research. Don't let your emotions get in the way. Don't blindly follow analysts and media financial commentators. When you decide to buy a stock or mutual fund, put your reasons down on paper. Periodically, review your rationale to see if your reasons for buying the stock still stand up.

➤ Get in the habit of regularly reading a good financial publication, such as the *Wall Street Journal, Barron's, Investor's Business Daily,* and *Business Week.*

➤ Check out independent research sources. Morningstar, Value Line, and Standard & Poor's are among the best.

➤ You'll grow rich slowly by sticking with an automatic investment plan that includes buying high quality, dividend-paying stocks and index funds on a regular basis.

CHAPTER 10

Bonds and Your Portfolio

B onds don't carry the glamour and excitement of stocks or their profit potential, but they have their place in most investment programs. They provide diversification, a certain amount of stability, and income for those seeking to supplement their living expenses. Bonds are especially attractive to retirees because of the steady stream of income, which is why they're often referred to as *fixed-income investments*.

Although bonds historically have had lower long-term returns, they have not been anywhere near as volatile as stocks. In this chapter, we'll look at the different types of bonds, their positives and negatives, and how they can be best used in investment portfolios.

First, a simple definition of what a bond is. When you buy a bond, you're loaning money to the entity that issued it. The entity can be a corporation, the U.S. government, or state and local governments. When you purchase a bond, you don't have an ownership interest, as you do when you buy stock.

In return for the use of the money you loaned the entity by purchasing its bond, the company agrees to pay interest to you at a stated rate, which is the *coupon rate*. When the loan is paid back at the end of the agreed-upon time period—in investment lingo, when the bond "matures"—the issuer repays the investor's principal.

Types of Bonds

Corporate bonds are among the riskiest—because of the uncertainty associated with running a business—while government bonds are among the safest, since they're backed by the full faith and credit of the U.S. government. The risks associated with government agency bonds—such as the mortgage lenders Federal National Association (Fannie Mae) and Federal Home Loan Mortgage Association (Freddie Mac)—and municipal bonds vary, but they usually fall in between the risks of corporate and government bonds.

Municipal bonds, which are issued by state, county, or city governments, are exempt from federal tax and are generally state tax-free for residents of the state in which they're issued. A "muni" that's free of federal, state, and city taxes is known as *triple tax-free.*

Because they're attractive to high-income investors, triple tax-free munis generally offer a lower coupon rate than equivalent taxable bonds. Depending on the investor's tax rate, though, the return may be higher than on a regular bond. To calculate the tax-equivalent yield for someone in the highest federal tax bracket of 35 percent, divide the coupon yield, say 3.5 percent, by one minus 0.35, or 0.65 (the formula is tax-exempt yield divided by one minus tax bracket). This gives a hypothetical tax-equivalent yield of 5.4 percent, and it would be boosted by any state and local tax deduction.

For those in high-income tax states, there's a list of recommended single-state munis in the Appendix.

You can also buy bonds via bond mutual funds, which provide diversification at a lower cost than buying many different individual bonds. These funds come in different varieties as well, including corporate, municipal, and government.

Credit Rating Agencies

Bonds carry credit, market, and interest rate risks. Credit risk is the risk that the bond issuer will default before the bond reaches maturity. If so, you may lose some or all of the principal amount you invested and any outstanding income that is due. If you need to sell your bond before its maturity date and the bond's price has dropped, you'll lose part of your principal investments as well as the future income stream. That's the market risk, or price fluctuations. The third leg of the risk stool—interest rate risk—refers to the fact that when interest rates increase, the price of a bond will usually fall. The reverse is true too: When interest rates fall, the price of the bond will typically rise.

Bonds are rated by different agencies, with Standard & Poor's and Moody's the biggest in the field. Standard & Poor's top rating is AAA, and Moody's is Aaa. The ratings run the gamut from triple A through D (in payment default). To use Standard & Poor's language, they are based on the issuer's likelihood of payment, the nature and provisions of the obligation and protection afforded by the bond, and relative position of the obligation in the event of bankruptcy, reorganization, or other arrangement under the laws of bankruptcy and other laws affecting creditors' rights.

Under commercial bank regulations issued by the Comptroller of the Currency, bonds rated in the top four categories (Standard & Poor's AAA, AA, A and BBB, commonly known as investment-grade ratings) are generally regarded as eligible for bank investment. Also, the laws of various states governing legal investments impose certain ratings or other standards for obligations eligible for investment by savings banks, trust companies, insurance companies, and fiduciaries in general. See S&P's Bond Ratings table, Figure 10-1.

If you own an individual bond and plan to hold it until maturity, you don't have to be overly concerned about market risk and interest rate risk. If you're in a bond mutual fund, however, you have to factor in these two risks because fund managers can buy

---

FIGURE 10-1 S&P's Bond Rating Categories

Investment-Grade Bonds

AAA	highest quality
AA	high quality
A	high medium-grade
BBB	medium-grade

High-Yield, or Junk Bonds

BB	uncertain outlook
B	generally lacking desirable qualities
CCC	poor quality, danger of default
CC	very speculative, may be in default
D	in default

and sell bonds as often as they feel it necessary to meet the fund's objective. As a result, you risk loss because of fluctuations in the fund's value.

Callable Bonds

Callable bonds can be redeemed by the issuer prior to the stated maturity date at the issuer's discretion. The bonds may be called on specific dates only, or periodically on notice to investors. Callable bonds usually are issued by companies with high credit ratings and offer you higher yields than comparable noncallable bonds to compensate for the increased risk that your bonds will be "called in." Maturities may be as short as three years and as long as 30 years. Generally these bonds are called in when interest rates are declining, which means investors have to reinvest their principal at lower rates.

Here's an example of this reinvestment risk:

An investor buys a 10-year corporate bond that is callable in two years with a 6 percent interest rate, while a 10-year non-callable Treasury security has a 4 percent interest rate. Two years later, the interest rate for a 10-year Treasury security has declined to 2 percent. The drop in interest rates prompts the corporation to call in its 6 percent bond and take advantage of the lower rates by issuing new bonds. If the former owner of the 6 percent callable corporate bond wants to buy another bond, the interest rates are lower than those available two years ago. So not only has the investor had the 6 percent corporate bond called away, but by taking the risk of purchasing that callable bond, the investor gave up the opportunity to purchase a noncallable 4 percent Treasury security, which would have continued to provide interest payments, while the drop in interest rates would have also resulted in a rise in the value of the security.

The bottom line: Be sure when you buy an individual bond that you find out whether it is callable, and if it is, the callable date.

Treasury Securities

Treasury securities, which include Treasury bills, notes, and bonds, generally are not callable prior to maturity. The exception: Before 1985 the Treasury issued marketable, callable long-term bonds, and many of them are still outstanding. A positive is that Treasury securities are exempt from state and local taxes, though Uncle Sam still has to get paid his share.

Treasury bills, or T-bills, mature in one year or less from the issue date. You buy T-bills for a price less than their par (face) value, and when they mature you're paid at their par value. Your interest is the difference between the purchase price of the security and what you are paid at maturity (or what you get if you sell the bill before it matures). If, for example, you bought a $10,000 26-week T-bill for $9750 and held it until maturity, your interest would be $250. The minimum amount that you can purchase of any given Treasury bill or note is $1000. Additional amounts must be in multiples of $1000.

Treasury notes are securities that pay a fixed rate of interest every six months until they mature, which is when you're paid their par value. These notes mature in more than a year but not more than 10 years from their issue date. You usually can buy Treasury notes for a price close to their par value.

There are two kinds of notes: fixed principal and inflation-indexed. Both pay interest twice a year, but the principal value of inflation-indexed securities is adjusted to reflect inflation as measured by the consumer price index. With inflation notes, your semiannual interest payments and maturity payment are based on the inflation-adjusted principal value of your security.

The 10-year Treasury inflation-indexed notes introduced in 1997 are called Treasury Inflation Protection Securities, or TIPS. Their main drawback is that you have to pay taxes each year on the compensatory additions to principal, even though you don't actually see the money until you redeem the security. Mutual funds that invest in the securities are required to pay you the adjustment for inflation each year, but taxes are still owed. This type of fund with the lowest expense ratio, at 0.25 percent, is the Vanguard Inflation-Protected

Securities Fund. In the year ending December 31, 2002, the fund's average annual return was 16.6 percent, and since inception in June 2000, it was 12.1 percent.

The other inflation-indexed security—the inflation-protected U.S. Savings Bond (known as the I Bond)—is not only exempt from state and local taxes, but is not federally taxable until it's redeemed, which can be as many as 30 years away. The return on the I Bond, which was introduced in September 1998, is based on two rates: a fixed rate that lasts for up to 30 years, and a rate based on inflation that is adjusted every six months (November 1 and May 1).

You can buy the bonds through banks—not brokers—in denominations ranging from $50 to $10,000. They can also be purchased for $1000 at a time via the website www.savingsbonds.gov. An individual can purchase no more than $30,000 worth of the bonds per calendar year. One drawback to the bonds is that they are pieces of paper that the investor is responsible for safekeeping. They cannot be held in a brokerage account. The Bureau of the Public Debt will replace lost, stolen, or destroyed bonds if the holder can provide the serial number, issue date, and taxpayer identification.

The I Bonds are purchased at face value, with no sales charge, and can be redeemed beginning after six months. The issue date is the month and year when payment is received by the issuing agent. Designed as a long-term savings vehicle, the bonds have a penalty for early redemption. An I Bond redeemed within the first five years loses three months of earnings. So a bond redeemed at 18 months will pay 15 months of earnings. Under certain circumstances, returns on the bonds are federally tax exempt if the proceeds are used to pay college tuition and fees.

The Treasury Department has created a program called the Savings Bond Wizard, available at www.savingsbondwizard.com, that helps investors keep track of their holdings. The Wizard shows your bond inventory in a spreadsheet format. The program includes these features: It (1) displays the current value and interest rate for each bond; (2) checks for valid combinations of serial number, series, denomination, and issue date; (3) shows the yield to date, next accrual date, and final maturity date for each bond; (4) recalculates bond values and interest for different redemption dates; and (5) allows for an update of the bond database every six months.

Zero Coupon Bonds

Zero coupon bonds don't pay interest during the life of the bond. They are bought at a deep discount to the maturity value. For example, you might pay $650 today to get back $1000 in five years. The difference between what you pay now and what you receive in the future is your return. "Zeros" are similar in concept to savings bonds.

The bonds, also known as STRIPS (Separate Trading of Registered Interest and Principal of Securities), are taxable each year on how much income has accrued, so even though you receive no cash, you still have to pay tax. Some investors prefer zero coupon bonds and zero coupon bond funds to save for specific goals, such as retirement or a child's college education, because they can estimate in advance about how much these investments will be worth when they mature.

TreasuryDirect

All Treasury securities are issued in "book-entry" form, which is an entry in a central electronic ledger. You can hold Treasury securities in one of two systems: TreasuryDirect or the commercial book-entry system.

TreasuryDirect (website: www.treasurydirect.gov) is a direct holding system where you have a direct relationship with the Treasury. The commercial book-entry system is an indirect holding system where you hold your securities with your financial institution, government securities broker, or dealer. This system is a multilevel arrangement that involves the Treasury, the Federal Reserve System (acting as the Treasury's agent), banks, brokers, dealers, and other financial institutions. You will pay fees under the commercial book-entry system, but unlike TreasuryDirect, you can use the securities as collateral and also hold zero coupon bonds.

TreasuryDirect makes payments by direct deposit to your bank account and sends statements directly to you. There are no fees when you open an account or buy securities. TreasuryDirect also allows you to automatically reinvest most maturing securities.

Ginnie Maes

Ginnie Mae securities are pools of loans to low- and moderate-income homeowners. The loans are mainly made under programs run by the Federal Housing Administration (FHA), which is part of the Department of Housing and Urban Development, and by the Department of Veterans Affairs (VA). The securities are known as pass-through instruments because the principal and interest payments flow to investors from the underlying pool of mortgages. Ginnie Mae guarantees the timely payment of principal and interest, so there is no credit risk attached to these investments. The best way to invest in Ginnie Maes is via mutual funds.

The main risk with Ginnie Maes—as with all mortgage instruments (Fannie Mae and Freddie Mac)—is prepayment risk. If interest rates go down, and the fixed cost of refinancing is reasonable, borrowers will seek better deals, as we've seen in spades from 2001 to 2003. As higher rate loans disappear from the portfolio, Ginnie Mae funds must reinvest their assets in lower-yielding loans. As a result, investors in the funds can expect the yield on their investment to go down. Ginnie Maes, like all fixed-income investments, also carry interest rate risk: As rates go up, the prices of the bonds go down.

Ginnie Mae securities offer the full faith and credit of the United States, unlike the other guarantors of mortgage loans, Fannie Mae and Freddie Mac, which are government-sponsored enterprises that secure qualifying conventional home loans.

By far the largest Ginnie Mae fund is offered by Vanguard. Its expense ratio is only 0.25 percent, while the average annual return for the year ending December 31, 2002, is 9.7 percent; for three years, 9.6 percent; five years, 7.3 percent; 10 years, 7.2 percent; and since inception (June 1980), 9.5 percent. Fidelity also has a large Ginnie Mae fund, with an expense ratio of 0.60 percent and the following average annual total return track record: one year ending December 31, 2002, 7.8 percent; three years, 9.3 percent; five years, 6.7 percent; and 10 years, 6.6 percent.

High-Yield, a.k.a. Junk, Bonds

Bonds that have a well-above-average yield may seem attractive to the novice, but as with all investments, the higher the return, the more risk is involved. The reason issuers have to pay a high yield, to quote Shakespeare, is that "something is rotten in the state of Denmark." The entities offering these bonds have no choice but to pay a high yield because their financial condition is thought to be weak. The rating agencies recognize these problems and thus accord the company or municipality a "below investment grade" credit rating.

High-yield bonds—also known as "junk bonds"—are much more volatile than investment-grade bonds. In addition to the high credit risk—and the usual interest-rate risk associated with all bonds—junk bonds are highly susceptible to economic downturns. When the economy is weakening, investors stay away from the bonds of companies that might not be able to pay interest or principal if their business is affected by the poor business conditions.

Michael Milken's name often comes to mind when discussing junk bonds. Milken was dubbed the "junk bond king" back in the 1980s because of his strategy of financing corporate takeovers with high-yield bonds. He made a fortune for himself and his employer, Drexel Burnham Lambert. In 1989, however, a grand jury indicted Milken for violations of federal securities and racketeering laws. He pleaded guilty to securities fraud and related charges in 1990, and the government dropped the more serious charges of insider trading and racketeering. The "junk bond king" was dethroned and sentenced to prison for 10 years, though in 1991 his sentence was reduced to two years plus three years probation.

Since these bonds are so risky, if you want to speculate and buy them, you're better off purchasing them through a well-diversified mutual fund, which will do the work of credit analysis and diversification for you. If you buy an individual junk bond, you risk losing everything if it defaults. Default rates have averaged 4 percent annually for the past 20 years, but in 2002 the rate more than doubled. Some recommendations: T. Rowe Price High Yield (Symbol: PRHYX, Telephone: 800-638-5660), Buffalo High Yield (Symbol: BUFHX, Telephone: 800-492-8332), and Columbia High Yield (Symbol: CMHYX, Telephone: 800-547-1707).

The Yield Curve

The yield curve is a good indicator of where one can get the most attractive yields. Simply, it's a graphic representation of the relationship between yield and maturity of securities. The curve, whose shape changes over time, shows the relationship between yield and maturity at a certain moment in time. The fixed-income securities plotted on the yield curve must have common characteristics, such as the same credit risk and the same tax treatment.

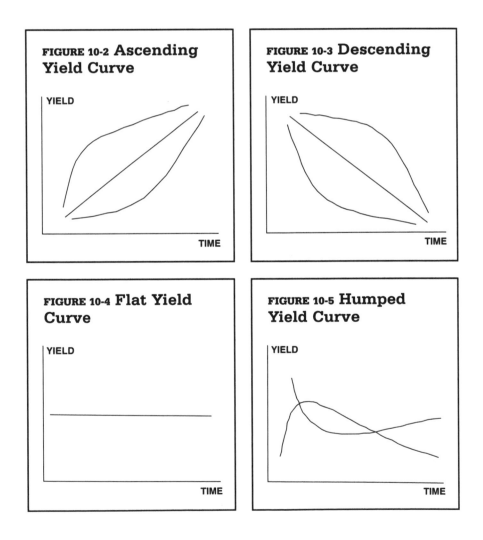

FIGURE 10-2 Ascending Yield Curve

YIELD

TIME

FIGURE 10-3 Descending Yield Curve

YIELD

TIME

FIGURE 10-4 Flat Yield Curve

YIELD

TIME

FIGURE 10-5 Humped Yield Curve

YIELD

TIME

Usually, short-term bonds carry lower yields because they're considered less risky. Yields of longer-term bonds are higher, since there's more risk that something will go wrong along the way before a 15- or 20-year bond matures. Thus, a normal yield curve (see Figure 10-2) slopes gently upward as maturities lengthen and yields rise, a depiction that shows short-end maturities paying less than the intermediates, and the intermediates paying less than the long-term bonds.

When bond investors expect the economy to be healthy without significant changes in inflation rates, the yield curve is normal, since investors who risk their money for longer periods expect to get higher yields than those whose money is at risk for shorter periods. If the curve slopes up steeply, you might use the barbell strategy (see point number 2 in the Reducing Risk list below). See Figure 10-3.

A flat yield curve (Figure 10-4) generally offers much the same yields at each level. In this situation, you would seek the highest yield for the lowest risk.

Sometimes the yield curve is inverted; that is, yields on long-term bonds are lower than those on short-term bonds. The reason? Longer-term investors are content with lower yields if they think rates are going even lower in the future because of a possible recession. This can well be a signal that the price of short-term bonds will fall. See Figure 10-5.

Reducing Risk

Here are some strategies to help reduce your risk when you invest in bonds:

1. Match your investment time horizon to the maturity of your investments. If, for example, you need to withdraw interest plus $5000 in principal from your portfolio each year to help meet living expenses, buy bonds or bond funds with maturities of one, two, and three years in $5000 increments. Depending on your time frame, you can then invest a portion of your remaining portfolio in intermediate bonds (five to 10 years), which typically pay a higher interest rate.

2. Buy for the long term both short- and long-term maturities (this is called the "barbell approach" and will help reduce investment risk).

3. Buy bonds and bond funds with average maturities all along the maturity spectrum but with the heaviest concentration in shorter-term bonds. This so-called "laddering" will help reduce fluctuations in value. For example, in a 10-year laddered portfolio, you might purchase bonds that mature in one, two, three, four, five, six, seven, eight, nine, and 10 years. When the first bond matures in a year, you would reinvest in a bond that matures in 10 years, and so on for each year.

Laddering

Here's an example of laddering: If you're in early retirement and have $80,561 to invest, you might purchase 10 zero-coupon Treasury bonds and notes, each with a face value of $10,000, scheduled to mature in one to 10 years. This would give you a portfolio with an average maturity of 5.5 years (the sum of each maturity divided by 10 rungs).

As the principal comes due each year, you would reinvest in another Treasury with a face value of $10,000 due to mature in 10 years, preserving the 5.5-year average maturity. Based on consensus interest rate expectations over the next 10 years, this portfolio would generate cash flow of $44,880 over 10 years, or $4488 per year. The yield to maturity on this cash flow would be 5.56 percent. Assuming the money is spent rather than reinvested, the ending market value of the portfolio after 10 years would be $72,434. Reinvesting the cash flow each year would, of course, increase the ending value of the portfolio and the portfolio's total annualized return, estimated at 3.68 percent.

In addition to generating a stream of income, staggered maturities also provide liquidity, or access to your principal at intervals, without having to sell into the market. And you avoid locking yourself into a single maturity for a long period of time.

For example, if you invested all your money in 10-year Treasuries that yield around 4.5 percent, and interest rates start moving upward, you would miss out on the higher yields and the opportunity to invest in lower-priced bonds (remember, as interest rates rise, bond prices fall). By the time your bonds come due, interest rates could even be heading downward again. In a declining interest rate environment, the laddered portfolio would mitigate your reinvestment risk because only a small portion of it is being rolled over each year (see Figure 10-6).

FIGURE 10-6. **Laddered Treasury Bond* Portfolio. Based on current consensus interest rate expectations over next ten years.**

Security	Maturity Date	Maturity Value	Current Price	% Yield to Maturity
1-year	2/1/04	$10,000	$9,817	1.86%
2-year	2/1/05	10,000	9,604	2.04
3-year	2/1/06	10,000	9,229	2.71
4-year	2/1/07	10,000	8,825	3.17
5-year	2/1/08	10,000	8,423	3.49
6-year	2/1/09	10,000	8,007	3.77
7-year	2/1/10	10,000	7,530	4.14
8-year	2/1/11	10,000	7,103	4.37
9-year	2/1/12	10,000	6,814	4.35
10-year	2/1/13	10,000	6,350	4.65

Beginning Market Value of Portfolio $80,561
Total Cash Flow† from Portfolio $44,880
Ending Market Value of Portfolio over 10 Years....................$72,434
Total Annualized Return..3.68%
Average Annual Cash Flow Yield 5.56%

*Securities are Zero-Coupon (Strips)
†Cash flow includes incremental net proceeds realized from rolling over bonds at lower prices.

Source: Standard & Poor's.

Points to Remember

➤ There are many different kinds of fixed-income investments and different strategies to help you diversify and allocate your portfolio. Yes, bonds are boring, but they can play an important role in your financial plan. Bonds don't carry the glamour or the profit potential of stocks, but they have their place in most investment programs. And they are less volatile than stocks over the longer term.

➤ When you buy a bond, you're loaning money to the entity (corporation, government, or municipality) that issued it.

➤ Municipal bonds, which are issued by state, county, or city governments, are exempt from federal tax and are generally state-tax-free.

➤ Bonds can be purchased via bond funds, which provide diversification at a lower cost than buying many different individual bonds.

➤ Bonds, which are rated by different agencies, carry credit, market, and interest rate risks.

➤ Callable bonds may be redeemed by the issuer prior to the stated maturity date at the issuer's discretion. Make sure when you buy a bond if it is callable, and be aware of the earliest date it can be called away.

➤ Treasury securities include Treasury bills, notes, and bonds. There are also inflation-indexed notes (called TIPS) and inflation-indexed U.S. Savings Bonds (I Bonds).

➤ You can buy Treasury securities via TreasuryDirect (www.treasurydirect.gov).

➤ Zero coupon bonds are bought at a deep discount to the maturity value.

➤ Ginnie Mae securities, which are pools of loans to low- and moderate-income homeowners, offer the full faith and credit of the United States and therefore don't have any credit risk.

➤ High-yield bonds, also known as junk bonds, are speculative and should be purchased only through mutual funds.

➤ The yield curve is a good indicator of where one can get the most attractive yields. The curve shows the relationship between yield and maturity at a certain moment in time. Usually, short-term bonds carry lower yields because they're less risky.

➤ Strategies to reduce fixed-income risk include matching your investment time horizon to the maturity of your investments, buying for the long term both short- and long-term maturities (the barbell approach), and buying bonds with average maturities all along the maturity spectrum but with the heaviest concentration in shorter-term bonds (laddering).

CHAPTER 11

The Seventh Key: Start Now

W e've all heard the many maxims about time. Time is of the essence. Time is money. Time waits for no man; or to be politically correct, no person. No time like the present.

In the investment world, though they might be clichés, these adages are particularly apt. Time is probably the most important factor in a successful long-term investment program. To paraphrase another old saw: "The early bird gets the fattest returns." The earlier you get started, the better chance you have of enjoying a comfortable retirement, sending the kids through college, buying your dream house or car, or attaining whatever goal you want to meet. It can't be emphasized enough how important it is to get started early. You'll see why in the following examples.

Fred started investing $200 a month at age 25. Ten years later, he stopped because he needed the money to support his growing family. When he reached 65, he nevertheless had amassed $402,797. He earned an average annual return of 8 percent on his investment.

By contrast, Fredwina didn't start investing until she was 35. She, too, invested $200 a month. But she didn't stop after 10 years, as Fred did. She contributed $200 monthly for 30 years. Her average annual rate of return was the same as Fred's: 8 percent.

Fredwina, at age 65, however, wound up with only $300,059. That's $102,738 less than Fred, even though she invested $200 a month for 30 years, or $72,000, and Fred invested the same amount per month for only 10 years, or $24,000.

What gives here?

The answer is simple. Fred's 10-year head start gave his account the fuel it needed to grow on its own. The magic of compounding comes into play here. We began talking about compounding in the first chapter, and now here's more on the subject.

The Magic of Compounding

As we have learned, compounding simply means that earnings on your investments generate earnings themselves in the form of interest, dividends, or capital gains. Over a period of years, that effect snowballs and can help your investments grow even faster.

Consider this example: If an investment returns 8 percent a year and its earnings are reinvested annually, your total return after one year will be 8 percent. After five years, your cumulative total return will be 47 percent. After 10 years, your cumulative total return will be 116 percent.

In money terms, an investment of only $100 a year earning 8 percent will grow to $7311 in 25 years, compounded annually. You will have invested only $2500 in that time, but your earnings will total $4811. That's an annual average return of 23.4 percent. If you invested $100 annually at a 10 percent rate, it would be worth nearly $10,000 in 25 years, for an average return of more than 39 percent annually.

Reinvestment is the key to compounding. Most investments permit you to take your earnings in cash rather than reinvesting them. If you cash out your earnings, however, you don't allow the magic of compounding to work for you. You would also have to pay taxes and/or have other penalty costs.

Legendary banker Baron Edmond de Rothschild called compounding the eighth wonder of the world. And as we mentioned in an earlier chapter, Albert Einstein said compound interest is the most powerful force on earth. Who could possibly disagree with these two geniuses?

Starting Early Makes a Big Difference

To fully benefit from compounding, you have to start early. The sooner you begin your investment plan, the greater the compounding effect. If a 20-year-old's objective is to amass $1 million by his or her 60th birthday, he or she needs to invest $1148 a year earning a 12 percent annual return. But someone who waits until age 40 needs to invest $12,070 a year. As this example points out, for the early bird, most of the wealth is generated by growth of the investment.

Archimedes, the renowned Greek mathematician and inventor, said, "Give me a lever long enough, and I can move the earth." In investing, time is that lever, and if you give yourself enough of it, you won't have to worry about eating cat food in your old age.

It's easy to make excuses as to why you can't start saving and investing now. You need a new car. Your pet cockatoo needs surgery. You got a great deal on a Las Vegas vacation. The stock market is too high. The stock market is depressed. Unfortunately, one of our human foibles is to put off today what we think we can do tomorrow.

Can you say "discipline"? For the sake of your financial future, you've got to force yourself to start your investment program now.

If your goal is to amass $1 million down the road, and you start at age 25, you would have to invest only $179 a month at an annual return of 10 percent for 40 years to reach the million-dollar mark. If you wait until 35, your monthly investment would have to jump to $481 for 30 years to reach $1 million by 65. If you further postpone your investment program until age 45, you must sock away $1382 monthly for 20 years to amass your million.

You can see the tremendous difference between starting at age 25 versus age 45 to meet your money goal. By waiting 12 years, you have to invest $1203 more each month.

If you fail to start early, you'll either have to save much more money every year, work longer than you'd hoped to, or else live on the edge when you retire.

As we said, there's no time like the present. That should be your mantra. If you start early and follow the six other keys in this book, you cannot fail to meet your financial goal.

Points to Remember

➤ Time is a critical factor in a successful long-term investment program.

➤ Compounding really works its magic, especially given an early start date.

➤ Begin now.

➤ No excuses.

Appendix

Recommended Mutual Funds

As discussed in this book, I believe no-load, low expense ratio index funds are the best way to go for the average investor. There are more than 5,000 managed equity mutual funds (up from 665 in 1985), and the vast majority don't beat the market indexes, and if they do, it's a hit or miss proposition. At the same time, the high expense ratios and sales commissions imposed by managed funds eat into your returns. I also have included some non-index funds for further diversification. Here are my favorites.

Vanguard 500 Index Fund Investor Shares (Symbol: VFINX)

Objective: Seeks to track the investment returns of the S&P 500 index. Provides a convenient way to match the performance of a substantial portion of the nation's largest stocks.

Telephone: (800) 662-2739

Website: www.vanguard.com

Investment minimum: $3,000

IRA: $1,000

Subsequent investments: $100

Expense ratio: 0.18%

Peers' expense ratio: 1.31%

Average annual total return (as of 12/31/2002):
1 year: –22.15%; 3 year: –14.60%; 5 year: –0.61%; 10 year: +9.27%; since inception (8/31/1976): +11.88%.

Vanguard Total Stock Market Index Fund Investor Shares (Symbol: VTSMX)

Objective: Seeks to track the investment returns of the Wilshire 5000 Total Market Index, which includes virtually all regularly traded U.S. stocks. Fund provides a convenient way to match the performance of the entire U.S. stock market.

Telephone: (800) 662-2739

Website: www.vanguard.com

Investment minimum: $3,000

IRA: $1,000

Subsequent investments: $100

Expense ratio: 0.20%

Peers' expense ratio: 1.31%

Average annual total return (through 12/31/2002):
1 year: –20.96%; 3 years: –14.3%; 5 years: –0.80%; 10 years: +8.60%; since inception (4/27/1992): +9.04%.

T. Rowe Price Equity Index 500 Fund (Symbol: PREIX)

Objective: Seeks to match the performance of the S&P 500 index, which is made up of primarily large-cap companies that represent a broad spectrum of the U.S. economy and about 70% of the U.S. stock market's total capitalization.

Telephone: (800) 225-5132

Website: www.troweprice.com

Investment minimum: $2,500

IRA: $1,000

Subsequent investments: $100 (IRA, $50; systematic purchase minimum, $50)

Expense ratio: 0.35%

Peers' expense ratio: 1.31%

Average annual average return (through 12/31/2002):
1 year: –22.21%; 3 years: –14.75%; 5 years: +0.83%, 10 years: +9.01%, since inception (3/1990): +9.79%

T. Rowe Price Total Equity Market Index Fund (POMIX)

Objective: Seeks to match the total return of the entire U.S. stock market as represented by the Wilshire 5000 equity index. Because the largest stocks carry the most weight in the index, large-cap stocks make up a substantial majority of the Wilshire 5000's value.

Telephone: (800) 662-2739

Website: www.troweprice.com

Investment minimum: $2,500

Subsequent investments: $100

IRA: $1,000 (to add to an IRA account: $50)

Systematic purchase minimum: $50

Expense ratio: 0.40%

Peers' expense ratio: 1.31%

Average annual return (through 12/31/2002:
1 year: –16.58%; 3 years: –0.6%; 5 years: +2.73%; since inception (9/94: +12.99%).

TIAA-CREF Managed Allocation Fund (TIMAX)

Objective: Seeks capital appreciation by investing in several of the other TIAA-CREF mutual funds. About 60 percent of its assets will be invested in shares of the TIAA-CREF International Equity, Growth Equity and Growth & Income funds, while about 40 percent are invested in shares of the Bond Plus, Short-Term Bond or High-Yield Bond Funds.

Telephone: (800) 223-1200

Website: www.TIAA-CREF.org/mfs

Investment minimum: $1,500

IRA: $500

Systematic purchase minimum: $50

Expense ratio: 0.39%

Peers' expense ratio: 1.29%

Average annual total return (through 12/31/2002):
1 year: −12.09%, 5 years: +2%; since inception (9/1997): +16.37%.

Vanguard Asset Allocation Investors Fund (VAAPX)

Objective: Seeks to provide long-term total return commensurate with an investment in an all-stock fund, but with less risk. A computer model is used to evaluate expected returns and risks of stocks, bonds and money market securities, which helps to determine changes in allocation.

Telephone: (800) 662-2739

Website: www.vanguard.com

Investment minimum: $3,000

IRA: $1,000

Subsequent investments: $100

Expense ratio: 0.42%

Peers' expense ratio: 1.29%

Average annual total return (through 12/31/2002):
1 year: −15.8%, 3 years: −5.62%; 5 years: +2.09%; since inception (11/1988): +10.79%

Recommended Mutual Funds for More Conservative Investors

Vanguard Wellesley Income Fund Investor Shares (Symbol: VWINX)

Objective: Seeks current income and moderate long-term capital growth by investing 60% to 65% of its assets in high-quality intermediate- and long-term corporate bonds and U.S. government securities with an average maturity of 5 to 15 years, and 35% to 40% in the stocks of established, dividend-paying companies. This fund's conservative strategy aims to provide a high and sustainable income stream consistent with moderate risk.

Telephone: (800) 662-2739

Website: www.vanguard.com

Investment minimum: $3,000

IRA: $1,000

Subsequent investments: $100

Expense ratio: 0.30%

Peers' expense ratio: 1.29%

Average annual return (through 12/31/2002):
1 year: +4.64%; 3 years: +9.29%; 5 years: +6.96%; 10 years: +10.03%; since inception (7/10/1970): +11.08%.

T. Rowe Price Equity Income Fund (Symbol: PRFDX)

Objective: Seeks to provide substantial dividend income, as well as long-term capital appreciation, through investments in common stocks of established companies.

Telephone: (800) 225-5132

Website: www.troweprice.com

Investment minimum: $2,500

IRA: $1,000 (to add to an IRA account: $50)

Systematic purchase minimum: $50

Expense ratio: 0.78%

Peers' expense ratio: 1.38%

Average annual return (through 12/31/2002):
1 year: −13.04%; 3 years: −0.10%, 5 years: +2.54%
10 years: +10.90%; since inception: (10/31/1985): +12.76%

Dodge & Cox Balanced Fund (Symbol: DODBX)

Objective: Seeks long-term growth of principal and income. A secondary objective is to achieve a reasonable current income.

Telephone: (415) 981-1710

Website: www.dodgeandcox.com

Investment minimum: $2,500

IRA: $1,000

Subsequent investments: $100

Expense ratio: 0.53%

Peers' expense ratio: 1.28%

Average annual return:
For the 10-year period ending 12/31/2002: 12% vs. 9.3% for the S&P 500 and 7.8% for the balanced fund peer group.

Vanguard Balanced Index Fund (Symbol: VBINX)

Objective: Seeks current income and long-term capital growth by investing 60% of its assets in stocks tracking the Wilshire 5000 Total Market index (which represents the entire U.S. stock market) and 40% bonds tracking the Lehman Aggregate Bond index (which represents the entire U.S. bond market). The fund maintains a fixed asset mix regardless of market conditions.

Telephone: (800) 662-2739

Website: www.vanguard.com

Investment minimum: $3,000

IRA: $1,000

Subsequent investments: $100

Expense ratio: 0.22%

Peers' expense ratio: 1.2%

Average annual return (through 12/31/2002):
1 year: –9.52%; 3 years: –4.92%; 10 years: +8.3%; since inception (11/1992): +8.63%.

Vanguard Total Bond Market Index Fund Investor Shares (Symbol: VBMFX)

Objective: Seeks current income by investing in a mix of bonds—corporate, government, and mortgage-backed—that represents the total universe of public investment-grade bonds in the U.S. that have maturities over one year. The fund, which tracks the Lehman Aggregate Bond Index, maintains an average maturity of 5 to 10 years.

Telephone: (800) 662-2739

Website: www.vanguard.com

Investment minimum: $3,000

IRA: $1,000

Subsequent investments: $100

Expense ratio: 0.22%

Peers' expense ratio: 1.00%

Average annual total return (through 12/31/20021):
1 year: +8.26%, 3 years: +9.35%, 5 years: +7.10%, 10 years: 7.26%, since inception (12/1986): +7.78%.

Recommended Mutual Funds for More Aggressive Investors

These funds are for the more stout-hearted who are willing to take on higher risk for potentially well-above-average gains.

T. Rowe Price Small-Cap Stock (Symbol: OTCFX)

Objective: Seeks to provide long-term capital growth by investing primarily in stocks of small companies. While investing in small- to medium-sized companies is generally riskier than investments in more established companies, it may offer greater capital appreciation potential.

Telephone: (800) 225-5132

Website: www.troweprice.com

Investment minimum: $2,500

IRA: $1,000

Subsequent investments: $100

Expense ratio: 0.98%

Peers' expense ratio: 1.47%

Average annual return:
1 year: -14.2%, 3 years: +2.20%, 5 years: +3.40%, 10 years: +11.32, since inception (6/1956): +13.45%.

Vanguard Small-Cap Value Index Fund (VISVX)

Objective: Seeks to track the investment returns of the S&P SmallCap 600/BARRA Value index with the lowest price-to-book value ratio. The fund provides a convenient way to match the performance of a diversified group of small value companies.

Telephone: (800) 662-2739

Website: www.vanguard.com

Investment minimum: $3,000

IRA: $1,000

Subsequent Investments: $100

Expense ratio: 0.27%

Peer's expense ratio: 1.57%

Average annual total return:
1 year: −14.20%, 3 years: +5.94%, since inception (5/1998): 1.59%.

CGM Focus Fund (Symbol: CGMFX)

Objective: Focuses on equity investments in a smaller number of companies and/or in a more limited number of sectors than diversified mutual funds. Flexibly managed with the ability to invest in equity, debt and fixed income securities, in different industry sectors and in foreign securities.

Phone: (800) 343-5678

Website: www.cgmfunds.com

Investment minimum: $2,500

IRA: $1,000

Subsequent investments: $50

Expense ratio: 1.20%

Peers' expense ratio: 1.57%

Average annual return (through 12/31/2002):
1 year: –17.79%, 3 years: +23.17%, 5 years: +16%, since inception (9/1997): +13.55%

Recommended No-Load, Low-Expense-Ratio Municipal Bond Funds (Single-State)

Those in high federal tax brackets and in states with high tax rates should consider investing in single-state municipal bonds that are free of federal, state, and local taxes. These are among the best:

(Arizona) American Century AZ (Symbol: BEAMX)

Telephone: 800-378-9878

Minimum initial investment: $5,000

(California) American Century CA Ins TF (Symbol: BCINX)

Telephone: 800-378-9878

Minimum initial investment: $5,000

(California) Fidelity Spartan CA Muni (Symbol: FCTFX)

Telephone: 800-544-8544

Minimum initial investment: $10,000

(California) Vanguard CA Long-Term Tax Exempt (Symbol: VCITX)

Telephone: 800-662-2739

Minimum initial investment: $3,000

(Florida) T. Rowe Price FL Muni (Symbol: FLTFX)

Telephone: 800-638-5660

Minimum initial investment: $2,500

(Florida) Vanguard FL Long-Term Tax Exempt (Symbol: VFLTX)

Telephone: 800-662-2739

Minimum initial investment: $3,000

(Georgia) T. Rowe Price Tax Free GA Bond (Symbol: GTFBX)

Telephone: 800-638-5660

Minimum initial investment: $2,500

(Maryland) Fidelity Spartan MD Income (Symbol: SMDMX)

Telephone: 800-544-8544

Minimum initial investment: $10,000

(Maryland) T. Rowe Price Tax Free MD Bond (Symbol: MDXBX)

Telephone: 800-638-5660

Minimum initial investment: $2,500

(Massachusetts) Fidelity Spartan MA Muni (Symbol: FDMMX)

Telephone: 800-544-8544

Minimum initial investment: $10,000

(Minnesota) Fidelity Spartan MN Muni (Symbol: FIMIX)

Telephone: 800-544-8544

Minimum initial investment: $10,000

(New Jersey) T. Rowe Price Tax Free NJ Bond (Symbol: NJTFX)

Telephone: 800-638-5660

Minimum initial investment: $2,500

(New Jersey) Vanguard NJ Long Term Tax Exempt (Symbol: VNJTX)

Telephone: 800-662-2739

Minimum initial investment: $3,000

(New York) T. Rowe Price Tax Free NY Bond (Symbol: PRNYX)

Telephone: 800-638-5660

Minimum initial investment: $2,500

(New York) USAA Tax Exempt NY Bond (Symbol: USNYX)

Telephone: 800-531-8722

Minimum initial investment: $3,000

(New York) Vanguard NY Long Term Tax Exempt (Symbol: VNYTX)

Telephone: 800-662-2739

Minimum initial investment: $3,000

(North Carolina) Dupree NC Tax Free Income (Symbol: NTFIX)

Telephone: 800-866-0614

Minimum initial investment: $100

(Ohio) Fidelity Spartan OH Muni (Symbol: FOHFX0)

Telephone: 800-544-8544

Minimum initial investment: $10,000

(Ohio) Vanguard OH Long Term Tax Exempt (Symbol: VOHIX)

Telephone: 800-662-2739

Minimum initial investment: $10,000

(Oregon) Columbia OR Muni Bond (Symbol: CMBFX)

Telephone: 800-547-1707

Minimum initial investment: $1,000

(Pennsylvania) Fidelity Spartan PA Muni (Symbol: FPXTX)

Telephone: 800-544-8544

Minimum initial investment: $10,000

(Pennsylvania) Vanguard PA Long Term Tax Exempt (Symbol: VPAIX)

Telephone: 800-662-2739

Minimum initial investment: $3,000

(Tennessee) Dupree TN Tax Free Income (Symbol: TNTIX)

Telephone: 800-866-0614

Minimum initial investment: $100

(Virginia) USAA Tax Exempt: Virginia Bond (Symbol: USVAX)

Telephone: 800-531-8722

Minimum initial investment: $3,000

Recommended Exchange-Traded Funds (ETFs)

An exchange-traded fund, or ETF, is a basket of stocks, usually based on an index. Investors can get in and out of these shares anytime at a price close to their net asset value (NAV), which is helpful when the market is skidding. Mutual fund holders, by contrast, can only get out of their investments at the closing price on any day. Also, the expense ratios of ETFs are typically about half those of similar mutual funds. ETF commissions, though, make them impractical replacements for no-load mutual fund shares purchased by dollar cost averaging. And you can't buy ETFs via automatic investment plans. Here are the more appealing ones, all traded on the American Stock Exchange:

S&P 500 SPDRS (Standard & Poor's Depositary Receipts), or Spiders (Symbol: SPY). Tracks the Standard & Poor's 500 index.

S&P MidCap 400 (Symbol: (MDY). Tracks the Standard & Poor's MidCap 400 index.

S&P SmallCap 600 (Symbol: IJR). Tracks the Standard & Poor's SmallCap 600 index

iShares S&P 500 (Symbol: IVV). Marketed by Barclays Global Investors. Tracks the Standard & Poor's 500 index.

iShares Russell 3000 (Symbol: IWV). Marketed by Barclays Global Investors. Tracks the Russell 3000 index.

Diamonds (DJIA Diamonds Trust, Symbol: DIA). Tracks the Dow Jones Industrial Average.

Recommended Direct Stock Purchase Plans

Stocks you can buy directly from companies are a good way to invest for the long term. Direct Purchase Plans not only save you commissions, but they also allow you to set up an automatic investment plan, which enforces discipline and, at the same time, you get the benefits of dollar cost averaging. Following are some of my favorite plans. The stocks all carry a high Standard & Poor's Quality ranking, which shows S&P's appraisals of the growth and stability of earnings and dividends over the past 10 years. To obtain enrollment forms, call the toll-free numbers or go online.

AFLAC (Symbol: AFL)

Telephone: (800) 227-4756

Website: www.aflac.com

AFLAC is the leading marketer of supplemental insurance products in the U.S. and Japan. From its origins in the mid-1950s as a provider of cancer insurance, the company has expanded its product offerings to include an array of supplemental health insurance products designed to help pay out-of-pocket expenses not covered by primary insurance.

Standard & Poor's Quality Ranking: A+

Plan minimum to join: $1,000

Optional cash payments of $50 per investment to $120,000 annually; stock is purchased bimonthly.

Automatic investment services available.

Bank of America (Symbol: BAC)

Telephone: (888) 279-3457

Website: www.bankofamerica.com

Formed through the 1998 merger of North Carolina-based Nations-Bank and California-based BankAmerica Corp., Bank of America is a bank holding company that provides a range of banking and financial services and products to 30 million households and 2 million businesses. The company has leading deposit market shares in California, Florida, Georgia, and Maryland.

Standard & Poor's Quality ranking: A–

Plan minimum to join: $1,000

Optional cash payments of $50 to $120,000 annually; stock is purchased weekly.

Automatic investment services available.

Duke Energy (Symbol: DUK)

Telephone: (800) 488-3853

Website: www.duke-energy.com

Duke provides electric service to about 2 million customers in North and South Carolina, and is one of the largest U.S. transporters and marketers of natural gas. In 2002, the company completed the acquisition of Vancouver-based Westcoast Energy, which has about $10 billion in assets, primarily related to natural gas gathering, processing, storage, and distribution.

S&P Quality ranking: A–

Plan minimum to join: $250

Optional cash payments of $50 to 100,000 monthly; stock is purchased bimonthly.

Automatic investment services available.

ExxonMobil (Symbol: XOM)

Telephone: (800) 252-1800

Website: www.exxon.mobil.com

ExxonMobil, formed through the merger of Exxon and Mobil in late 1999, is the world's largest publicly owned integrated oil company. The company serves customers in more than 200 countries and has an ownership interest in 46 refineries in 26 countries, with 6.3 billion barrels of distillation capacity a day. ExxonMobil's geographically diversified base and balance between exploration and production and refining and marketing are big plusses.

S&P Quality ranking: A–

Plan minimum to join: $250

Optional cash payments of $50 to $200,000 annually; stock is purchased weekly.

IRA option is available.

Automatic investment services available.

Federal Home Loan (Symbol: FRE)

Telephone: (800) 519-3111

Website: www.freddiemac.com

This company, known as Freddie Mac, is a U.S. government-sponsored enterprise that buys mortgages from lenders in order to increase the supply of funds for housing. In its portfolio business, Freddie Mac functions in a manner similar to a savings and loan that originates home mortgage loans to hold for its own account. The major differences are that Freddie Mac uses capital market borrowings to finance its mortgage purchases, whereas thrifts use retail savings, and that Freddie Mac purchases mortgages from various lenders, while thrifts actually issue mortgages to homebuyers.

S&P Quality ranking: A+

Plan minimum: $250 (or automatic monthly investments of at least $50 for five consecutive months)

Optional cash payments of $25 minimum; stock is purchased weekly.

Automatic investment services available.

General Electric (Symbol: GE)

Telephone: (800) 786-2543

Website: www.ge.com

This industrial and media behemoth is also one of the world's largest providers of financing and insurance. GE makes large utility generators, locomotives, lighting products, aircraft engines, medical diagnostics equipment, and plastics. The NBC broadcast network is also part of the mix.

S&P Quality ranking: A+

Plan minimum: $250

Optional cash payments of $10 to $10,000 per transaction; stock is purchased weekly.

Automatic investment services available.

Home Depot (Symbol: HD)

Telephone: (800) 774-4117

Website: www.homedepot.com

Founded in 1978, Home Depot is the world's largest home improvement retailer, and the second largest U.S. retailer after Wal-Mart. The company operates more than 1,400 stores that stock 40,000 to 50,000 items per store. With the 2001 acquisition of three residential construction flooring businesses, Home Depot became the largest supplier in a $12 billion market.

S&P Quality ranking: A+

Plan minimum: $250

Optional cash payments of $25 to $100,000 annually; stock is purchased weekly.

Automatic investment services available.

Johnson Controls (Symbol: JCI)

Telephone: (800) 524-6220

Website: www.johnsoncontrols.com

Johnson Controls, which goes back to 1885, is a leading maker of automotive interior systems, automotive batteries and automated building control systems. It also provides facility management services for commercial buildings. Current government building trends promoting facility management outsourcing and energy efficiency programs bode well for the company.

S&P Quality ranking: A+

Plan minimum: $250.

Optional cash payments of $50 to $15,00 per quarter; stock is purchased monthly.

Automatic investment services available.

Lowe's Companies (Symbol: LOW)

Telephone: (877) 282-1174

Website: www.lowes.com

Lowe's is the second largest U.S. do-it-yourself home improvement retailer after Home Depot. The company has grown from a chain of 15 stores in 1962 to more than 800 stores in 2002 in 43 states. Since 1989, Lowe's has been transforming its store base from a chain of small stores into a chain of home improvement warehouses. In 2003, it is expected to open more than 120 new stores.

S&P Quality Ranking: A+

Plan minimum: $250

Optional cash payments of $25 to $100 per month; stock is purchased monthly.

Automatic investment services available.

Omnicom Group (Symbol: OMC)

Telephone: (800) 870-2370

Website: www.omnicomgroup.com

This global advertising and marketing services company is one of the largest corporate communications companies in the world. Omnicom is comprised of more than 1,500 companies operating in more than 100 countries. It operates as three independent agency networks: the BBDO Worldwide Network, the DDB Worldwide Network, and the TBWA Worldwide Network.

Standard & Poor's Quality ranking: A+

Plan minimum: $250 (or automatic monthly investments of at least $75).

Optional cash payments of $75 to $120,000 annually; stock is purchased weekly.

Automatic investment services available.

Paychex (Symbol: PAYX)

Telephone: (800) 937-5449

Website: www.paychex.com

In fiscal 2002 (ended May), this provider of payroll processing, human resources and benefits services for small to medium-size businesses recorded its 12th consecutive year of record revenues and net income. Paychex has more than 100 locations and serves more than 390,000 clients. Its primary customers are firms that have less than 100 employees.

Standard & Poor's Quality ranking: A+

Plan minimum: $250

Optional cash payments of $100 to 10,000 monthly; stock is purchased weekly.

Automatic investment services available.

Pfizer (Symbol: PFE)

Telephone: (800) 733-9393

Website: www.pfizer.com

Pfizer traces it history back to 1849. With the acquisitions of rival drug makers Warner-Lambert in 2000 and Pharmacia Corp. in 2003, Pfizer is by far the world's largest prescription pharmaceuticals company. It spends more than $7 billion annually on research and development.

Standard & Poor's Quality ranking: A+

Plan minimum: $500

Optional cash payments of $50 to $120,000 annually; stock if purchased weekly.

Automatic investment services available.

Wal-Mart Stores (Symbol: WMT)

Telephone: (800) 438-6278

Website: www.walmartstores.com

Operating a chain of discount department stores, wholesale clubs and combination discount stores and supermarkets, Wal-Mart is the largest retailer in North America. The company has an annual technology and communications budget of more than $500 million and has long been a leader in developing and implementing retail information technology.

Standard & Poor's Quality ranking: A+

Plan minimum: $250 (or automatic monthly investments of at least $25).

Optional cash payments of $100 to $150,000 annually; stock is purchased weekly.

IRA option is available.

Automatic investment services available.

50 Companies with Largest Market Values in S&P 500

The S&P 500 is made up of large-capitalization stocks. Capitalization, as we've discussed, is the number of shares of a company outstanding times the price. Since I advocate investing in index funds, it's important to know what the larger-cap stocks are.

FIGURE A. 50 Largest Market Value Companies (Year End 2002)

	Ticker	Stock Name	Shares	Price per Share	Market Value (Mil. $)	% of 500	% Cumu-lative
1	MSFT	Microsoft Corp.	5,346,450,000	51.70	276,411,465,000	3.41	3.41
2	GE	General Electric	9,951,061,000	24.35	242,308,335,350	2.99	6.40
3	XOM	ExxonMobil	6,728,898,000	34.94	235,107,696,120	2.90	9.30
4	WMT	Wal-Mart Stores	4,413,963,000	50.51	222,949,271,130	2.75	12.05
5	PFE	Pfizer	6,162,164,000	30.57	188,377,353,480	2.32	14.37
6	C	Citigroup	5,136,268,000	35.19	180,745,270,920	2.23	16.60
7	JNJ	Johnson & Johnson	2,970,581,000	53.71	159,549,905,510	1.97	18.57
8	AIG	American Int'l. Group	2,608,595,000	57.85	150,907,220,750	1.86	20.43
9	IBM	Int'l Business Machines	1,690,088,000	77.50	130,981,820,000	1.62	22.05
10	MRK	Merck & Co.	2,245,556,000	56.61	127,120,925,160	1.57	23.61
11	PG	Procter & Gamble	1,299,299,000	85.94	111,661,756,060	1.38	24.99
12	KO	Coca-Cola Co.	2,479,113,000	43.82	108,634,731,660	1.34	26.33
13	VZ	Verizon Communications	2,735,763,000	38.75	106,010,816,250	1.31	27.64
14	BAC	Bank of America	1,496,699,000	69.57	104,125,349,430	1.28	28.92
15	INTC	Intel Corp.	6,625,000,000	15.57	103,151,250,000	1.27	30.20
16	CSCO	Cisco Systems	7,225,133,000	13.10	94,649,242,300	1.17	31.36
17	SBC	SBC Communications	3,320,203,000	27.11	90,010,703,330	1.11	32.47
18	MO	Philip Morris (Altria Group)	2,068,629,000	40.53	83,841,533,370	1.03	33.51
19	WFC	Wells Fargo	1,691,889,000	46.87	79,298,837,430	0.98	34.49
20	PEP	PepsiCo Inc.	1,727,045,000	42.22	72,915,839,900	0.90	35.38

	Ticker	Stock Name	Shares	Price per Share	Market Value (Mil. $)	% of 500	% Cumu- lative
21	VIA.B	Viacom Inc.	1,761,096,000	40.76	71,782,272,960	0.89	36.27
22	LLY	Lilly (Eli) & Co.	1,123,374,000	63.50	71,334,249,000	0.88	37.15
23	CVX	ChevronTexaco Corp.	1,068,157,000	66.48	71,011,077,360	0.88	38.03
24	UPS	United Parcel Service	1,116,585,000	63.08	70,434,181,800	0.87	38.89
25	DELL	Dell Computer	2,589,842,000	26.74	69,252,375,080	0.85	39.75
26	FNM	Fannie Mae	995,000,000	64.33	64,008,350,000	0.79	40.54
27	ABT	Abbott Labs	1,562,541,000	40.00	62,501,640,000	0.77	41.31
28	AMGN	Amgen	1,287,066,000	48.34	62,216,770,440	0.77	42.08
29	AOL	AOL Time Warner	4,470,147,000	13.10	58,558,925,700	0.72	42.80
30	ORCL	Oracle Corp.	5,355,934,000	10.80	57,844,087,200	0.71	43.51
31	HD	Home Depot	2,325,758,000	23.96	55,725,161,680	0.69	44.20
32	MDT	Medtronic Inc.	1,220,120,000	45.60	55,637,472,000	0.69	44.89
33	CMCSA	Comcast Corp.	2,308,006,000	23.57	54,399,701,420	0.67	45.56
34	PHA	Pharmacia Corp	1,292,917,000	41.80	54,043,930,600	0.67	46.22
35	HPQ	Hewlett-Packard	3,051,466,000	17.36	52,973,449,760	0.65	46.88
36	WYE	Wyeth	1,325,651,000	37.40	49,579,347,400	0.61	47.49
37	WB	Wachovia Corp.	1,360,308,000	36.44	49,569,623,520	0.61	48.10
38	MMM	3M Company	390,197,000	123.30	48,111,290,100	0.59	48.69
39	BLS	BellSouth	1,858,564,000	25.87	48,081,050,680	0.59	49.29
40	JPM	J.P. Morgan Chase	1,996,511,000	24.00	47,916,264,000	0.59	49.88
41	AXP	American Express	1,314,319,000	35.35	46,461,176,650	0.57	50.45
42	BMY	Bristol-Myers Squibb	1,937,045,000	23.15	44,842,591,750	0.55	51.00
43	MWD	Morgan Stanley	1,085,622,000	39.92	43,338,030,240	0.53	51.54
44	ONE	Bank One Corp.	1,164,609,000	36.55	42,566,458,950	0.53	42.06
45	DD	Du Pont (E.I.)	993,480,000	42.40	42,123,552,000	0.52	52.58
46	BUD	Anheuser-Busch	855,905,000	48.40	41,425,802,000	0.51	53.09
47	FRE	Federal Home Loan Mtg.	695,706,000	59.05	41,081,439,300	0.51	53.60
48	USB	U.S. Bancorp	1,915,563,000	21.22	40,648,246,860	0.50	54.10
49	TYC	Tyco International	1,995,175,000	17.08	34,077,589,000	0.42	54.52
50	FITB	Fifth Third Bancorp	577,788,000	58.55	33,829,487,400	0.42	54.94

Long-Term Dividend-Paying Stocks

During the severe bear market of 2000–2002, investors rediscovered the merits of stocks that pay dividends. In many cases, dividend-paying stocks not only provide a steady stream of income but also maintain better price stability. That's because during such times investors seek the relative safety associated with long-time dividend payers. Each of the companies in this table has paid dividends for at least 27 years and each has boosted its payments for at least 25 years in a row.

FIGURE B. **Companies in the S&P 500 Index That Have Boosted Their Dividends Consistently***

Company	Paid Each Year Since	Sector
3M Co.	1916	Industrials
Abbott Laboratories	1926	Health Care
ALLTEL Corp	1961	Telecommunication Services
Altria Group†	1928	Consumer Staples
AmSouth Bancorp	1943	Financials
Anheuser-Busch Cos.	1932	Consumer Staples
Archer-Daniels-Midland	1927	Consumer Staples
Automatic Data Processing	1974	Industrials
Avery Dennison Corp.	1964	Industrials
Bank of America	1903	Financials
Bard (C.R.)	1960	Health Care
Becton, Dickinson	1926	Health Care
CenturyTelephone Inc.	1974	Telecommunication Services
Chubb Corp.	1902	Financials
Clorox Co.	1968	Consumer Staples
Coca-Cola Co.	1893	Consumer Staples
Comerica Inc.	1936	Financials
ConAgra Foods	1976	Consumer Staples
Consolidated Edison	1885	Utilities
Donnelley (R.R.) & Sons	1911	Industrials
Dover Corp	1947	Industrials
Emerson Electric	1947	Industrials
Family Dollar Stores	1976	Consumer Discretionary

Company	Paid Each Year Since	Sector
First Tenn National	1895	Financials
Gannett Co.	1929	Consumer Discretionary
General Electric	1899	Industrials
Grainger (W.W.)	1965	Industrials
Heinz (H.J.)	1911	Consumer Staples
Household International	1926	Financials
Jefferson-Pilot	1913	Financials
Johnson & Johnson	1944	Health Care
Johnson Controls	1887	Consumer Discretionary
KeyCorp	1963	Financials
Kimberly-Clark	1935	Consumer Staples
Leggett & Platt	1939	Consumer Discretionary
Lilly (Eli)	1885	Health Care
Lowe's Cos.	1961	Consumer Discretionary
Masco Corp.	1944	Industrials
May Dept Stores	1911	Consumer Discretionary
McDonald's Corp.	1976	Consumer Discretionary
McGraw-Hill Companies	1937	Consumer Discretionary
Merck & Co.	1935	Health Care
Nucor Corp.	1973	Materials
PepsiCo Inc.	1952	Consumer Staples
Pfizer Inc.	1901	Health Care
PPG Indus	1899	Materials
Procter & Gamble	1891	Consumer Staples
Regions Financial	1968	Financials
Rohm & Haas	1927	Materials
Sigma-Aldrich	1970	Materials
Stanley Works	1877	Consumer Discretionary
Supervalu Inc.	1936	Consumer Staples
Target Corp	1965	Consumer Discretionary
TECO Energy	1900	Utilities
U.S. Bancorp	1930	Financials
VF Corp	1941	Consumer Discretionary
Wal-Mart Stores	1973	Consumer Discretionary
Walgreen Co	1933	Consumer Staples

*Cash payments based on ex-dividend dates from January 1 to December 31 of each year.
†Formerly Philip Morris Cos.

Standard & Poor's Quality Rankings As An Investment Tool

Standard & Poor's has provided earnings and dividend Quality rankings on common stocks since 1957. These rankings (A+, highest; A, high; A-, above average; B+, average; B, below average; B-, low; C, lowest; D, in reorganization) reflect the long-term growth and stability of a company's earnings and dividends. An S&P study on its Quality rankings has shown the following:

Over the 1985–2002 period, portfolios of stocks with high Quality rankings outperformed the S&P 500 Index and substantially outperformed portfolios of stocks with low Quality rankings. The portfolio with the highest quality (A+) outperformed the S&P 500 index by almost two percentage points.

Portfolio risk, as measured by standard deviation, is lower for higher Quality-ranked companies.

Fundamental risk is lower in portfolios of stocks with companies carrying high Quality rankings. The portfolios exhibit stable and persistent earnings, high returns on equity, stable and wide profit margins, and low debt levels.

Companies with high Quality rankings appear less likely to engage in accounting manipulations. Over the 1985–2002 period, these companies reported significantly lower non-recurring items. High Quality-ranking companies have higher quality of earnings as defined by S&P Core Earnings methodology. (See Chapter 2.)

Portfolios of stocks with high Quality rankings provide a cushion in down markets. Over the 1985–2002 period, these portfolios significantly outperformed the S&P 500 and portfolios of low Quality-ranked companies in times of general earnings deceleration and increasing credit risk.

Earnings growth for companies with high Quality rankings is not correlated with overall corporate earnings and credit cycles. Conversely, earnings growth for low Quality-ranking companies is more dependent on earnings and credit cycles.

FIGURE C. Market-Weighted Annual Returns for S&P Quality Ranking Portfolios

Year	A+	A	A-	B+	B	B-	C & Below	A+ A, & A-	B+, B, & B-	S&P 500
1986	3.1	8.3	4.7	3.8	-6.6	-6.5	-23.7	5.2	-1.1	4.0
1987	3.9	3.6	4.6	-1.5	10.6	8.8	7.7	3.9	3.9	5.2
1988	16.5	18.2	15.9	16.4	18.3	23.7	24.0	16.8	18.1	16.6
1989	26.4	34.2	36.3	22.5	24.1	18.9	24.3	32.2	22.4	31.6
1990	6.2	2.2	-6.9	-10.2	-15.0	-21.7	-10.2	0.2	-14.2	-3.1
1991	49.1	26.5	23.1	32.6	24.0	22.4	26.5	32.4	27.6	30.4
1992	2.4	2.8	11.7	12.7	15.7	13.9	16.1	5.5	13.9	7.6
1993	-2.9	5.2	10.2	12.3	25.4	29.1	20.0	4.0	20.2	10.1
1994	4.6	3.5	-2.8	-1.8	-0.6	-1.1	-7.4	1.6	-1.2	1.3
1995	42.7	35.2	34.8	31.5	37.1	30.0	26.7	38.1	33	37.5
1996	23.3	20.3	13.3	22.8	28.4	23.7	8.0	19.5	25.1	22.9
1997	37.0	42.7	31.7	29.4	28.5	26.2	19.0	37.2	28.4	33.4
1998	31.9	15.6	22.9	25.3	23.0	14.6	62.3	24.3	22.7	28.6
1999	14.5	1.9	2.1	33.1	27.0	30.3	103.4	7.7	30.1	21.0
2000	4.3	11.6	0.5	-10.2	-12.3	-16.9	-28.9	4.3	-12.2	-9.1
2001	-10.2	-2.4	-1.4	-15.8	-13.4	0.0	-27.6	-5.1	-12.5	-11.9
2002	-21.1	-17.6	-12.3	-19.7	-32.0	-20.0	-38.8	-17.3	-24.8	-22.1
$10,000 Invested	69,887	63,196	52,035	46,651						
Compound Return	12.3	11.6	10.3	9.5	9.0	8.9	7.1	11.5	9.1	10.8
Standard Deviation	16.1	14.5	14.6	17.4	19.0	20.0	29.1	14.4	18.0	16.1
Return/ Risk	0.77	0.80	0.71	0.54	0.47	0.45	0.24	0.80	0.51	0.67
Beta	0.91	0.81	0.82	1.04	1.09	1.09	1.36	0.85	1.07	
Alpha	2.42	2.64	1.46	-1.40	-2.26	-2.00	-4.58	2.04	-1.95	
Skewness	-0.43	-0.78	-0.67	-0.94	-0.98	-1.07	-0.27	-0.68	-1.06	-0.82

Recommended Websites

If you haven't already discovered for yourself, the Internet is a wonderful research tool. It has revolutionized and simplified the once arduous task of getting in-depth information on a subject. Here are some highly useful Websites:

www.google.com. This is by far the best search engine. Just type in a few words on the topic you're interested in, and up pops a wealth of information.

www.moneycentral.msn.com. Well written personal finance article and lots of stock market data. Lively, easy-to-understand market commentaries.

www.vanguard.com. The source for information on index funds. Has many other handy, useful investing features.

www.troweprice.com. The other mutual fund site that is a winner. Especially well done is the link to investment plan & tools.

http://finance.yahoo.com. This site will give you stock quotes, charts and a plethora of investment research. Yahoo's message boards on individual stocks are entertaining and sometimes enlightening.

www.morningstar.com. Good information on mutual funds and retirement planning. Some handy worksheets.

www.equityresearch.standardandpoors.com. This comprehensive site includes data on the Standard & Poor's indexes, independent stock research, fixed-income ratings, and mutual fund articles and ratings.

www.stockresearch.com. Independent research, stock quotes, educational articles, and links to other sites.

www.sec.gov, or the SEC's EDGAR (Electronics Data Gathering And Retrieval) data base. Companies' financial reports filed with the Securities and Exchange Commission are an excellent way to research a stock.

Index

About the Author

Formerly Managing Editor of Standard & Poor's investment advisory newsletter *The Outlook*, **Joseph R. Tigue** retired in early 2003 after nearly 25 years with the company. He is coauthor of *The Dividend Rich Investor*, which was picked as one of the best books of its type in print by *The New York Review of Books*. Tigue has been widely quoted on the stock market in newspapers around the nation and has frequently appeared on TV, including CNBC, CNN, PBS, and NBC. He is a graduate of New York University. Tigue was born in Pittston, Pennsylvania, and raised in Waterbury, Connecticut. He and his wife of 45 years live on Long Island. They are the proud parents of three daughters and are blessed with three grandchildren.